DYSLEXIA:
A TEENAGER'S GUIDE

DYSLEXIA:
A TEENAGER'S GUIDE

Dr Sylvia Moody

Vermilion
LONDON

7 9 10 8

First published in the United Kingdom in 2004 by Vermilion,
an imprint of Ebury Publishing

A Random House Group company

The Random House Group Limited Reg. No. 954009

Addresses for companies within the Random House Group can be found at
www.rbooks.co.uk

A CIP catalogue record for this book is available from the British Library

The Random House Group Limited supports The Forest Stewardship
Council (FSC), the leading international forest certification organisation.
All our titles that are printed on Greenpeace approved FSC certified paper
carry the FSC logo. Our paper procurement policy can be found at
www.rbooks.co.uk/environment

Printed and bound in Great Britain by
CPI Antony Rowe, Chippenham, Wiltshire

ISBN 9780091900014

To buy books by your favourite authors and register for offers visit
www.rbooks.co.uk

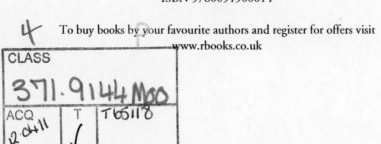

Contents

Acknowledgements

In writing this book I have greatly benefited from the
advice and support of my colleagues:

Diana Bartlett
Philomena Ott
Susan Close
Katherine Kindersley
Neil Milliken.

My grateful thanks to them.

Preface

A brief note to any teenagers picking up this book: if you have – or think you might have – dyslexic difficulties, you will find advice and guidance in this book on how to cope with them.

The first part explains exactly what dyslexic difficulties are, and how to go about getting them recognised and assessed. It also explains about a related group of difficulties called dyspraxia.

In the second part of the book there is advice on improving organisational, memory and literacy skills, and on dealing with negative emotions.

In the last part, there is advice about IT support and help organisations.

Although this book is written for you, the teenager, you might like to show it to your parents and teachers. It could help them to get a better understanding of your difficulties, and to find ways in which they could help and support you.

Also, if you have friends – dyslexic or not – who have problems with things such as essay writing or organising revision, you could get them to read Chapters 5–13 of this book. The advice given there could well be of help to them.

This book contains a lot of information, so I suggest you don't try to take it all in at once. Skim through the book to get a general idea of its contents, and then go back and read each chapter more carefully. The idea is to take on board the information and advice *gradually*.

I hope you will enjoy the book and find it useful.

Dr Sylvia Moody
Dyslexia Assessment Service
London

SECTION A

WHAT IS DYSLEXIA?

In this section I'll describe dyslexic difficulties in detail, and also explain how they relate to a similar set of difficulties called dyspraxia. From reading these descriptions you should be able to judge whether you are dyslexic or dyspraxic, or perhaps both.

I shall also explain how these difficulties can be assessed, and suggest some ways of making other people aware of your problems so they can give you help and support.

CHAPTER 1

Canterbury Tales

I'll begin by introducing you to two young people from Canterbury: Louisa and Paul. They are both at secondary school, and both have problems with school work that frustrate and baffle them. Here are their stories in their own words.

DYSLEXIA AND ME

Hello – my name is Louisa and I'm 17 years old. I live with my parents and my two younger brothers. I'm studying English, drama and history of art for A level. My two brothers, annoyingly, just sail through their school work, but I have all sorts of problems. I can explain them best by telling you about a typical school day.

My school day really begins the night before. Before I go to bed I have to look carefully at my timetable for the next day and make sure I have all the books I need for my different lessons. I've trained myself to do this over the years because otherwise, if I just try to get things together at the last minute in the morning, I'll be sure to forget something or take the wrong thing.

I usually walk to school with my friend Bettina, who lives a few doors away. She's also studying English and drama and we spend a lot of time together, both at school and outside it. We both belong to the local tennis club. We get to school a bit early so we can chat with our mates, and then lessons start at nine o'clock prompt.

Now the difficulties begin. And different lessons bring different difficulties.

In English the teacher sometimes asks us to read a passage to ourselves in class so that we can discuss it together. What I find is that everyone else has finished reading the passage and I'm still only halfway through it. I don't want to hold the whole class up, so I pretend I've read it all. This means I can't take part in the discussion. I'm trying to finish reading the passage and listen to what everyone's saying at the same time.

Sometimes we're asked to discuss a passage that we've read at home the night before. Two problems here: one is that I often find I can't really remember the passage, even though I spent hours reading it. Two is that, even if I remember the passage, I find it hard to get my thoughts on it together quickly enough to take part in the discussion. While I'm working out in my mind what I want to say, someone else says it – and in a much clearer way than I could.

This sort of thing happens all the time and it gets me really angry and frustrated. I feel I've got a lot of things inside myself – ideas, thoughts, opinions – but I just can't get them over to other people. It makes me feel stupid.

Maybe it's because I feel I can't express myself that I took up drama – to speak with someone else's voice. I'm quite good at acting, I think, but drama isn't just about acting, and there are quite a few things about it I find difficult. For a start, learning the lines. My memory is the pits and I often just blank out when we're performing. I feel a terrible sense of panic when that happens – my heart thumps and I go dizzy. It's like I've fallen into a black hole.

Our drama coach is quite sympathetic and often suggests I just read the lines in rehearsal. But I'm hopeless at reading aloud, too. I muddle up long words – I'll say something like hitotopamus for hippopotamus.

Then there's moving around on the stage. I'll be given a sequence of movements and I'll get them all muddled up. It seems I just can't win – whatever I try to do, there's always something to trip me up.

My other big problem is with writing, and I have to do a lot of that in my third subject, history of art. My spelling isn't *too* bad because I've worked hard at it, and my mum, who is a spelling supremo, has helped me with it. But my writing is a mess – not my handwriting so much, but the way I express my thoughts on paper. 'Jumble' is the word that comes to mind. I do know what I want to say but I find it hard to get started and I keep going off on tangents. I write and rewrite things but I'm never happy with them, and nor is my teacher. I should have done art, not history of art, because at least I am good at drawing.

It feels sort of embarrassing to talk about all these difficulties. Probably I sound like a real moaner and whinger, but I'd do anything not to have all these problems. I enjoy the subjects I do, I want to do well in them, I want to go to drama school and enjoy it. I don't want to be under pressure all the time. People say to me, 'What's your problem? You've got brains, you'll do okay.' But I just feel like screaming at them, 'I'm not okay, it's taking me hours to do things, I'm worn out, I'm in a muddle, something's not right – don't just make encouraging noises – find some way to help me.'

As you will gather, Louisa feels baffled and upset about her difficulties. Yet the pattern of difficulties she describes is quite common: it's usually termed 'dyslexia'.

PARENT ALERT
Early warning signs of dyslexia in your child
Late starting to talk.
Listens but doesn't hear.
Can't pronounce long words.
Can't remember instructions.

If, when you read Louisa's account of her difficulties, you felt her experiences were like your own, it's worth considering whether you, too, might be dyslexic.

Slow at reading?
Awful spelling?
Take forever to write an essay?
You could be dyslexic.

Let's look more closely both at the things Louisa does well and at the things that cause her difficulty.

Louisa is good at:
✓ Thinking about subjects that interest her
✓ Having ideas
✓ Forming opinions
✓ People skills – she has friends and enjoys chatting to them
✓ Acting
✓ Drawing
✓ Sport

Louisa is bad at:
- ✗ Reading aloud
- ✗ Reading for comprehension
- ✗ Explaining her thoughts clearly to people
- ✗ Structuring an essay
- ✗ Remembering things
- ✗ Following a sequence, e.g. movements on stage

There is a third category of things that Louisa is not naturally good at, but that she does reasonably well because she has managed to compensate for her difficulties to some degree.

Louisa has compensated for:
- Being disorganised – she checks the night before what she needs for school next day
- Poor spelling – she has worked hard on this with help from her mother

This, then, is a common dyslexic profile: good thinking power and perhaps some creative talent, but a variety of difficulties with literacy skills, expressing thoughts in words, memory, sequencing and organisation.

Everyday dyslexic problems
Counting change in shops.
Explaining things on the telephone.
Reading bus and train timetables.

Dyslexia is sometimes also called 'specific learning difficulty'. There are various types of specific learning difficulty, and in this book we shall mention one other type, called dyspraxia, which is closely linked to dyslexia.

Dyspraxia is basically a problem with physical coordination. But many dyspraxic people also have dyslexic difficulties, so there is a large overlap between the two syndromes. *For that reason all the advice given in this book will also be relevant to dyspraxic people.*

> **Everyday dyspraxic problems**
> Spilling drinks.
> Losing your way.
> Using keys and locks.

I shall now introduce you to Paul, who is dyspraxic. He will tell you in his own words about his difficulties. When you have read his account, you might like to compare the strengths and weaknesses he describes with those of Louisa. Try to see in which ways they are the same, and in which ways they are different.

DYSPRAXIA AND ME

Hi – I'm Paul. I'm 14 years old and I live in Canterbury with my mum, two dogs and a goldfish. My parents are separated, but my dad lives nearby and I see him most weekends. I go to the local school.

I'd like to say I enjoy school, but actually I don't. It's not so much the lessons – I get by with most things, if you don't count spelling and maths. The problem is more that I have some rather weird habits and people give me a hard time about them. I don't mean they actually bully me – I'm quite big, so they'd think twice about that – but they're always laughing at me and calling me names like 'Fall Guy'. Why? Because I do actually fall over a lot. I just trip over my feet and go sprawling on the floor and all my books come out of my bag and scatter everywhere.

Another thing is that I'm always bumping into things. I've lost count of the times I've hit my head against a door or banged my elbow on a desk. I've always got a bruise somewhere or other. Oh, yes – and I keep dropping things – like in the refectory my whole lunch often finishes up on the floor, or in science lessons I'm sure to drop a bottle of something – usually something that stinks horribly. As for sport, don't mention it. I am *not* wanted on team.

The whole of the school day is a sort of blur. I'm never quite sure what lesson I should be in or where it is, and even if I know the number of the classroom I'm going to, I can get hopelessly lost on the way and finish up in the wrong lesson. Even if I get to the right lesson, I usually find that I've got the wrong books with me, or I've forgotten something important.

My teachers get impatient with me. They say they tell me things again and again and I don't remember them – which is true. They say I don't do the right homework – which is true – usually because I didn't have time to copy it down properly from the board. My handwriting is very slow, and if I try to write fast, I can't read it back.

There are actually some things I'm good at – English, for instance. I like reading, and, if we're asked to write about a poem or a book we've read, I have lots of ideas and opinions I want to express. I write poetry myself, and I'd quite like to be a writer one day – though I have to admit that my writing, like the rest of my life, is a bit disorganised.

To be really honest with you, I'm tired of being the Fall Guy. I wish people at school could see how difficult life is for me and stop laughing at me. My dad says I should just ignore them and get on with my own life. I'll try to remember that the next time I'm flat on my back with my books spilling out all round me!

If you recognised yourself in Paul's account, maybe you should consider whether you are dyspraxic.

Always tripping over your feet?
Terrible sense of direction?
Can't read your own writing?
You might be dyspraxic.

Let's look more closely at the things Paul does well and the things he finds difficult:

Paul is good at:
- ✓ Reading
- ✓ Creative writing
- ✓ Thinking about things
- ✓ Having ideas
- ✓ Forming opinions

Paul is bad at:
- ✗ Maths
- ✗ Spelling
- ✗ Handwriting
- ✗ Remembering things
- ✗ Following a sequence, e.g. instructions
- ✗ Being organised
- ✗ Getting his bearings
- ✗ Keeping his balance
- ✗ Sport
- ✗ Making friends

So far, unlike Louisa, Paul hasn't managed to compensate for any of his difficulties, though he might do better at this as he gets older.

PARENT ALERT
Early signs of dyspraxia in your child
Late starting to walk.
Misses out crawling stage.
General clumsiness.
Problems with tying knots.

COMPARING DYSLEXIA AND DYSPRAXIA

Now you've heard both Louisa and Paul talk about what they're good and bad at, perhaps you can see that there are some things they both find difficult, and other things that cause problems for one but not the other. To show this more clearly, I've drawn up a table that directly compares the main difficulties reported by Louisa and Paul.

WHAT ARE THE DIFFICULTIES?

Activity	Louisa (dyslexic)	Paul (dyspraxic)
Reading	✗	
Spelling	(✗)	✗
Structuring written work	✗	✗
Remembering things	✗	✗
Following a sequence	✗	✗
Being organised	(✗)	✗
Maths		✗
Handwriting		✗
Keeping balance		✗
Getting bearings		✗
Playing sports		✗

A cross in brackets (X) indicates a difficulty that has been compensated for.

From this you can see that Louisa and Paul share several difficulties. The main differences between them are that Louisa is bad at reading but Paul is good at this: Paul has poor physical coordination, such as difficulty with handwriting and keeping his balance, whereas Louisa has no problems with these things; Paul is also bad at maths.

Earlier in the chapter I asked you to consider the difficulties reported by Louisa and Paul and to consider whether you, too, might be dyslexic or dyspraxic – or both. To help you decide better about this, this chapter ends with two questionnaires, one on dyslexia, one on dyspraxia.

If you did identify with Louisa or Paul, and if you tick yes to a lot of boxes in the questionnaires, perhaps you should consider getting yourself properly assessed so that you can get some specialist help for your difficulties. Assessment is further explained in Chapter 3.

ARE YOU DYSLEXIC?

Please tick the items that cause you difficulty.

READING
Reading quickly... ☐
Reading with good comprehension......................... ☐
Learning from books.. ☐
Recalling what has been read .... ☐
Reading for pleasure .... ☐

WRITING
Writing neatly... ☐
Writing quickly .... ☐
Dealing with reversible letters (b, d, p, q, m, w)............. ☐
Sequencing letters (was–saw)................................ ☐
Spelling.. ☐
Putting ideas down in writing............................... ☐
Filling in forms .... ☐
Writing a letter... ☐
Writing an essay... ☐

SPEECH AND COMPREHENSION
Saying long words... ☐
Speaking in public.. ☐
Explaining things to people simply and clearly .... ☐
Following conversations or discussions................. ☐
Taking notes in lessons.. ☐

MEMORY AND CONCENTRATION

Remembering and following instructions .... ❏

Remembering:

      messages .... ❏

      telephone numbers... ❏

      times of trains or buses...................................... ❏

      times of appointments .... ❏

Doing sums in your head... ❏

Concentrating for long periods .... ❏

Organising a study schedule/daily life .... ❏

PERCEPTION

Following left/right instructions .... ❏

Reading maps.. ❏

Finding your way in a strange place................................ ❏

Looking things up in dictionaries/directories................... ❏

EMOTIONAL REACTIONS

Please circle any of the following words or phrases that describe your reactions to your difficulties.

aggressive	depressed
angry	embarrassed
anxious	frustrated
confused	lacking in confidence
defensive	low in self esteem

ARE YOU DYSPRAXIC?

Please tick the items that cause you difficulty.

COORDINATION

Do you bump into things/people and often trip over?...... ☐
Do you often spill and drop things?.................................. ☐
Do you find it difficult to do practical tasks such as:
       cooking?.. ☐
       typing?.. ☐
       riding a bike? .... ☐
Do you find sports difficult, especially team games
  and bat and ball activities?... ☐

PERCEPTION

Do you have problems with:
       finding your way in a strange place?................... ☐
       following left/right instructions?........................... ☐
       telling the time on a clock face?........................... ☐
       reading a map?.. ☐
       judging distance and space? .... ☐
Are you over/under-sensitive to:
       sound? .... ☐
       touch?... ☐
       smell? .... ☐
       taste? .... ☐

MEMORY AND CONCENTRATION

Are you generally disorganised and untidy?..................... ☐
Do you find it hard to:
       remember and follow instructions? .... ☐
       do sums in your head? .... ☐
       concentrate for long periods? .... ☐
       take messages and pass them on correctly? .... ☐
       key in the correct numbers on the telephone?.... ☐
Do you mix up dates and times and miss appointments?.. ☐

Do you often lose things and not remember where you
have put them?.. ❏

SPEECH, LISTENING AND COMPREHENSION

Do you find it difficult to explain things to people
simply and clearly? .... ❏

When you say a long word, do you sometimes get the
sounds in the wrong order?.. ❏

Do you 'lose the thread' of conversations or discussions,
especially in groups?.. ❏

Do you sometimes blank out when talking to people?........ ❏

Do you find it difficult to take notes in lessons?.............. ❏

Is there a delay between hearing something and
understanding it? .... ❏

Do you find it difficult to interpret body language
(including facial expressions)? .... ❏

Do you often interrupt people?.. ❏

ORGANISATION

Do you have problems prioritising? .... ❏

Do you generally operate in a muddled way?.................... ❏

READING

Do you easily remember what you have read?.................. ❏

Do you lose your place when you are reading? .... ❏

Do words on a page seem to 'jump about'? .... ❏

WRITING

Is your handwriting untidy and difficult to read? .... ❏

Is your spelling poor, especially when under stress? .... ❏

Do you put letters and numbers in the wrong order? ..... ❏

Do you have difficulty putting your ideas down on
paper?.. ❏

Do you have problems with:
filling in forms?.. ❏
writing a letter? .... ❏

> organising and writing an essay?......................... ☐
> spotting spelling errors?.. ☐
> finishing off a piece of work?.............................. ☐

If you ticked quite a lot of the items in either or both of these questionnaires, you may well have dyslexic and/or dyspraxic difficulties.

If you have already been diagnosed as dyslexic or dyspraxic, you might still like to look at what you've ticked in the questionnaires to see if you knew that all the difficulties you've ticked were related to dyslexia or dyspraxia.

Some people are surprised that there are so many difficulties associated with dyslexia and dyspraxia. They find it hard to understand how they are all related to each other, and wonder what causes them. You'll find some answers to this in the next chapter.

CHAPTER 1 SUMMARY

In this chapter:
- ✓ Louisa told you about her dyslexic difficulties, and Paul told you about his problems with dyspraxia
- ✓ You were asked to think about what Louisa and Paul said and to see how far their difficulties, and their strengths, matched yours
- ✓ You filled in questionnaires about dyslexia and dyspraxia

---

CHAPTER 2

Understanding Dyslexia

In the previous chapter Louisa and Paul described a variety of difficulties they experience. In this chapter we'll look at the *underlying* problems in dyslexia and dyspraxia, and see how these affect both school work and life generally.

Note: From now on, as dyslexia and dyspraxia are so closely intertwined, I shall use the word dyslexia *most of the time* to cover both of them. However, some sections of the book will discuss particular aspects of dyspraxic difficulties separately.

Underlying areas of weakness
- Short-term memory
- Phonological skills (recognising, pronouncing and sequencing sounds)
- Sequencing and structuring information
- Perception
- Movement

We'll look at each of these separately.

SHORT-TERM MEMORY

Short-term memory (STM) is a *temporary* store for information. For example, we use STM to remember a telephone number for a few seconds while we key it in, or to keep the shape of an object in mind as we try to draw it. Once used, the information in the STM store will either be forgotten, or be transferred to our long-term memory store for future use.

Try this exercise in short-term memory

Carefully read through the following numbers ONCE ONLY, then look away and see if you can recall them in the correct order:

5 9 2 8 3 7 4 6

If you did remember all these numbers in the right order, your short-term memory is good.

One important part of STM is called 'working memory'. In the example given above, STM only had to remember information, not do anything with it. The working memory component, however, is active: it takes the information held in the main STM store and uses it in some way. For example, we use working memory when we do mental arithmetic.

Try this exercise in working memory

Carefully read the following arithmetic problem through ONCE ONLY, then try to work out the answer in your head.

Add 5 and 3 and 8 and 4, then divide by 2

Did you work out that the answer was 10? If so, your working memory is good.

Poor short-term memory causes problems with:
- Copying down numbers correctly
- Remembering messages, instructions and directions
- Keeping track of ideas when speaking, listening or writing
- Following the sense of a passage while reading it
- Taking notes from books
- Getting your thoughts in order when explaining things to people
- Saying long words
- Remembering dates
- Remembering names
- Remembering where things have been put
- Multi-tasking, such as listening to the teacher and taking notes

PHONOLOGICAL SKILLS
The term 'phonological skills' means our ability to deal with the sounds of our language. There are a number of things we have to do with sounds.

1. We have to be able to *recognise* them. When someone is talking to us, we need to know when they are making a **b** sound or a **z** sound, or whatever other letter sound they are making.
2. We need to be able to *pronounce* these sounds correctly ourselves.
3. We must be able to *distinguish* between similar sounds, e.g. to tell **p** from **b**, or **m** from **n**.
4. We need to *sequence* sounds correctly to make words. The longer the word, the harder it is to sequence the sounds. (Do you recall that Louisa said she muddled up sounds in long words, saying, for example, 'hitotopamus' for 'hippopotamus'?)

This difficulty with long words is usually due to a combination of poor phonological sequencing skill and poor short-term memory. You need to hold the sounds of a word in your memory while you get their sequence right.

Can you pronounce these words?
irresistible
irrepressible
contemporary
instantaneous
temporarily

Poor phonological skills cause problems with:
- Reading accuracy
- Spelling
- Saying long words
- Understanding long words

SEQUENCING AND STRUCTURING INFORMATION
Every time you want to describe or explain something to someone, every time you want to tell someone a story or a piece of gossip, you have to think just how you are going to present what you want to say. You have to decide how to begin, how to organise the information you're giving to the other person in a logical way – in other words, how to *structure* it.

In the previous section we talked about phonological sequencing, that is, getting the sounds of words in the right order. But this is only the beginning: you also need to be able to sequence words correctly in a sentence, and sentences in a paragraph. And when you're writing a whole essay, you have to think about how you're going to organise the various ideas you have about the subject of the essay. You need an introduction, then a logical sequence of ideas or arguments, and finally a conclusion. Again, you need a *structure*.

How does the sentence structure change the meaning?
Only *Mary* liked Bill.
Mary only *liked* Bill.
Mary liked *Bill* only.

It's not only in speaking and writing that we need structure. We often also find it useful to structure our time, in order to use it efficiently. Think of your school day: it's highly structured, with a timetable of lessons, and each individual lesson will be structured too. If you go on holiday, you probably make some sort of plan for each day's activities, so you get the right mix of sightseeing and relaxation.

Difficulty with sequencing and structuring information causes problems with:

- Writing and copying words and numbers accurately
- Following and understanding instructions
- Carrying out instructions in the correct sequence
- Structuring essays
- Taking clear notes
- Organising work and revision schedules
- Presenting an argument logically in a seminar
- Dealing with library catalogues
- Finding books
- Filing
- Carrying out tasks in an efficient, logical way

PERCEPTION

Perception is related to our five senses: vision, hearing, touch, taste and smell. When we perceive the world, we are using one or more of these senses (and perhaps also a sixth sense – intuition) to find out what is around us.

But perception involves more than using our sense organs (eyes, ears, nose, hands, tongue). Perception also uses the brain to understand the information the sense organs are receiving. For example, look at the illustration overleaf.

Source: Rubin's vase

What the eye sees is simply some black and white shapes. No more, no less.

The brain, however, is not satisfied with this. It looks for meaning in the shapes. First of all, the brain might decide the shapes show a black vase; after a moment's thought, however, it might think they could just as easily be two white human profiles.

In reaching decisions like this, the brain is not making random guesses. It is drawing on the stores of knowledge it has about human beings and the world we inhabit. It keeps such knowledge in a long-term memory store, which we all gradually build up from childhood onwards. Every time some information comes in from the sense organs, the brain tries to see how the information fits in with the knowledge it already has about the world. This helps the brain to understand and interpret the information correctly.

This, then, is perception: a collaboration between brain and sense organs to understand the world about us.

Let's turn now to something that dyslexic people find difficult: reading.

Reading obviously uses visual perception. Our eyes see letter shapes and our brain makes sense of them. But if your visual perception is poor, all sorts of problems can arise. For example, you might:

- See letters (or numbers) back to front, or upside-down, so you might mix up **m** and **w** or **p** and **b**
- See letters in the wrong sequence, so you might read **was** as **saw**
- Keep losing your place while reading
- Miss out words or lines
- Have difficulty keeping track of the letter sequence in a long word, so you might read **conversation** as **conservation**

Often, when the eye is having difficulty in keeping track of the letter sequence in a word, the brain tries to come to its aid. Say, for example, that the eye is struggling with the word **representing** and it has managed to inform the brain that certain letters are present, though it is not quite sure of the order. Maybe it has seen the letters **resning**. The brain immediately scans through its word store to try and match these letters to a word. It might come up with two or three suggestions (as with the vase or profile figure above). One of these might be the correct answer **representing**, but other possibilities could be **reasoning** and **resenting**. Often, but not always, context can help the brain to decide which is right.

Visual perception difficulties are by no means confined to reading. They cause all sorts of problems, some of them large-scale, such as finding your way about in a complex of buildings, some of them small-scale, such as dealing with mathematical material (graphs, geometrical shapes, diagrams, equations and tables of figures).

MOVEMENT

We noted in the first chapter that dyspraxic people have a particular difficulty with physical coordination. They find it hard to plan and execute movements – both small movements that we use for handwriting, and large movements that we make in, say, playing football.

These difficulties with movement are sometimes called 'motor difficulties'. Handwriting needs 'fine motor skills', while playing football needs 'gross motor skills'.

Difficulty with motor skills can cause:

- Slow and untidy handwriting
- Poor presentation of written work or figures
- Inaccurate keying on word processor, calculator or telephone
- General clumsiness or slowness
- Poor balance and posture
- Inability to play bat and ball games
- Poor judgement of distance
- Problems using machines, such as photocopiers
- Awkwardness carrying trays of mugs or dishes
- Tendency to fall, trip and bump into things and people

If these motor difficulties are severe, treatment to improve co-ordination can be obtained from physiotherapists or occupational therapists. Such treatment is outside the scope of this book, but more information about help for dyspraxic difficulties can be found on page 159.

WHAT NEXT?

Now you have some in-depth knowledge of dyslexic and dyspraxic difficulties, the next question is, 'What can be done about them?'

Well, the recommended first step is to have a formal assessment, and we shall discuss what this means in the next chapter.

CHAPTER 2 SUMMARY

In this chapter you learnt about the underlying problems in dyslexia and dyspraxia:
- ✓ Poor short-term memory
- ✓ Difficulty in pronouncing and sequencing sounds (phonological skills)
- ✓ Putting information into a good order or structure
- ✓ Seeing letters in the right order
- ✓ Coordinating movement

CHAPTER 3

Assessment

If, after reading the previous two chapters, you think that you might have dyslexic and/or dyspraxic difficulties, the next step would be to have an assessment by an expert. The word 'assessment' might sound daunting, but it's important to remember that it is not a test. There is no particular mark or level you have to reach, no pass or fail score.

WHAT'S THE PURPOSE OF ASSESSMENT?

The purpose of an assessment is to identify not only any difficulties you might have, but also your strengths. This is helpful because it will:

- Help you to decide what subjects you want to study in the future
- Provide a basis on which specialist help for your difficulties can be provided

WHAT HAPPENS IN AN ASSESSMENT

An assessment can be carried out by a psychologist or teacher who specialises in helping people with dyslexia or dyspraxia. The assessor will begin by talking to you about your difficulties, both at school and in daily life, and will then give you some tasks to see how you get on in different types of activity, including the following:

- Reasoning ability
- Memory
- Perception
- Movement or motor skill
- Phonological skills
- Literacy skills

ASSESSMENT TASKS

Below are some examples of the tasks you might be given.

Reasoning ability

1. Read the following:
Socks are to feet as gloves are to hands.

Now can you complete this one:
Ear is to radio as eye is to . . .

2. Read the following:
A robin and a canary are both types of bird.

Now can you say how the following are similar?
a) *Helicopters and aeroplanes*
b) *Sunshine and rain*
c) *Stamp-collecting and train-spotting*
d) *Museums and art galleries*

(Answers on page 34.)

Memory

You did some memory tasks in the last chapter. Here are a couple more.

1. Below is a sequence of mixed-up numbers and letters. Read through the sequence ONCE ONLY, then see if you can recall it.

5 M 9 A 2 T 7 S

2. You need a stopwatch or a clock with a second hand for this exercise. Below is a list of words. Give yourself ONE MINUTE ONLY to memorise them, then cover the list and try to recall all the words.

gnome
umbrella
spaniel
uncle
jelly
wizard
avenue
sunlight
grocer

A visual memory task could be to try and memorise a number of objects on a tray before they are covered over.

Perception
1. Your first task is to look at the following pairs of pictures and spot how they differ in certain details. In each pair there are five differences between the pictures (answers on page 34).

Louisa studies her script

Paul takes a teabreak

2. Your second task is to find a shape that has been 'hidden' in a complex pattern. For example, in this pattern, there is a hidden triangle. Can you spot it?

Now here are three similar exercises. In each case you are given the shape first and then a pattern in which it is hidden (answers on page 34).

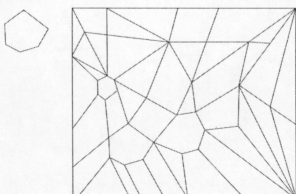

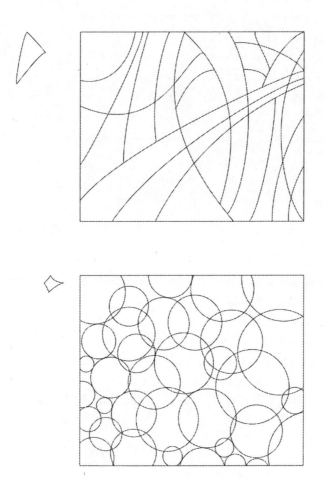

Movement or motor skill

You need a stopwatch or a clock with a second hand for this exercise.

Overleaf are some rows of symbols. Give yourself ONE MINUTE ONLY to copy as many as you can *onto a separate sheet*. Then check back carefully to see if you got them all right, especially if you got them the right way round. Or ask someone else to check if you don't trust yourself.

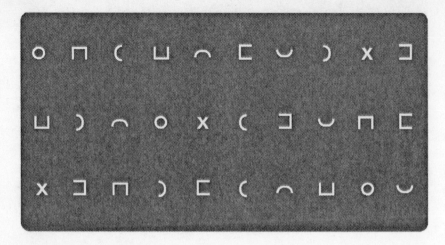

Phonological skills

You may remember that, in the previous chapter, I explained that phonological skill is the ability to recognise, pronounce and sequence sounds. You might therefore be asked to do a rather weird task, namely, read nonsense words. This stops you reading a word by just recognising it and forces you to concentrate on the sequence of sounds in the word.

You might get a list of nonsense words on their own, such as:

vob

scran

tiglup

colibity

extrompy

potaminously

Or you might be asked to read nonsense words mixed into a passage with real words, such as:

Once upon a time a triglop found a drub of magilicent bratebogs. 'Pallabaloo,' he cried, 'I've drooned my vellities at last. I'm utterly decabulous!'

Literacy skills

As well as all the general tasks described above, you'll be asked to do some reading, spelling, writing and, perhaps, maths. But again, these tasks are *not* tests that have a particular pass mark. You don't have to aim for any particular level. You just continue the tasks until you reach a point where they're becoming too difficult for you, and then stop.

Some people, even though they know an assessment isn't a test, feel quite nervous about it, and this is only natural. However, once the assessment gets going, they usually lose this anxiety, and by the end often feel quite happy and relieved to have got a greater understanding of themselves.

You may recall that, in Chapter 1, Louisa told you about the various difficulties she was experiencing. Eventually she spoke to one of her teachers about her problems, and the teacher, thinking it would be good to understand more about Louisa's difficulties, suggested an assessment. Rather nervously, Louisa agreed – and she didn't regret it.

Louisa's assessment

Louisa describes her assessment as follows:

'So – it was finally upon me: the day of the assessment. I'd been feeling vaguely nervous about it for weeks, and when it got to the night before, I felt really anxious. I don't know what about really. I suppose I felt I might make a complete fool of myself, or that there would be some dreadful revelations about me, or the psychologist would say, "You're a hopeless case, Louisa, never darken my door again."

'Mum and Dad kept saying there was nothing to worry about, but as we drove to the assessment, my hands felt clammy and my heart seemed to give little thuds. My brain had lost itself in a fog. Anyway, we got there, and Mum and Dad went off and left me with the psychologist, who was actually quite nice and friendly. He asked me all about my difficulties and explained the sort of tasks I would have to do to give him a full picture of my strengths and weaknesses.

'At first, I felt that my worst fears *were* being realised. I found it hard to give any sort of clear description of my problems; and, even though the tasks were quite straight-

---

forward, I could feel myself getting panicky and making a mess of simple things. The reading and writing bits were the worst; I could hear myself stumbling over words, and when I was asked to write a short composition, I just couldn't get started with it. As the assessment went on, though, I got more relaxed and things seemed to get easier.

'All the same, when we reached the end of the assessment I just sat there expecting to hear I'd completely messed up, so I was rather amazed when the psychologist explained to me that I had very good abilities generally. He said I also had some typical dyslexic weaknesses, but should be able to get round these if I got some help, and there was no reason why I shouldn't go on to drama school.

'I felt stunned for a few moments, then an overwhelming sense of relief. To my horror, I burst into tears – it seemed like all the years of frustration and worry about myself were suddenly pouring out.

'I felt embarrassed about being so emotional, though at the same time it made me feel a lot better. By the time Mum and Dad came back to collect me, I was in a really good mood. I felt as if a load had fallen off my shoulders. For the first time I felt sure that actually I was all right. I wasn't a hopeless case – I had some perfectly ordinary difficulties that I could get help for.

'So my advice to anyone who thinks they might be dyslexic is: get assessed. Since the assessment I have had one or two downbeat moments when I've felt angry about all the years I was struggling on without help or understanding. But mainly I feel very positive about the future, and I'm determined to do everything possible to deal with my difficulties and achieve all my ambitions in life. I'm looking forward not back.'

As you see from this first-hand account, although Louisa found the assessment a bit of an ordeal at first, she gained an enormous amount from it. In later months she would say it was the best day's work she had ever done.

Don't be disheartened if you are assessed and found to be dyslexic. Once your difficulties have been recognised you will be able to get help for them, and the more your particular dyslexic difficulties are tackled, the more your good abilities in other areas will be able to shine through.

AFTER THE ASSESSMENT

Being assessed isn't the end of the story. After an assessment two things need to happen:

1. The information gained in the assessment needs to be shared with family, friends and teachers so that everybody knows the situation.
2. A programme of help needs to be put in place. There is a lot you can do to help yourself, and I shall be giving you advice on this in Section B of this book. If possible, though, it's good to work with a specialist dyslexia teacher for a while so that you have someone on hand to advise and support you.

CHAPTER 3 SUMMARY

In this chapter you learnt:
✓ What happens in an assessment
✓ What sort of tasks you would do to assess:
  • reasoning ability
  • memory
  • perception
  • coordination of movement
  • phonological skill
  • literacy
✓ What emotions people can feel when they go for an assessment
✓ What happens after an assessment has been done

Answers

Reasoning ability (page 26)

1   television
2a   flying machines
2b   types of weather
2c   hobbies or pastimes
2d   places that display cultural objects

Perception (pages 27–29)

Spot the difference:

Hidden shapes:

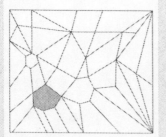 

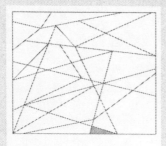 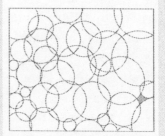

CHAPTER 4

Telling People
About Dyslexia

At the end of the last chapter we noted that, once you have had
an assessment and gained an understanding of your difficulties
and how they might be helped, you will need to give this information to various people. Of course, your parents or carers will
probably take a good deal of responsibility for this, discussing the
situation with other family members, your teachers and so on.

PARENT ALERT
How to support your child
Make sure your child's teachers are aware of the difficulties.
Watch out for signs of your child being
mocked or bullied at school.
Request extensions for homework projects.
Request concessions in examinations.

However, there will be many situations where you will need to take responsibility yourself for explaining the situation. For example, it could be that a particular teacher has not picked up on the fact that you have dyslexic difficulties, and is giving you a hard time about various things. Or perhaps someone in daily life might get impatient with you if, for instance, you're not taking in what they're telling you.

In these situations, you might want to alert the person to the fact that you sometimes need a bit of extra time to do things. Very often, just by saying something such as, 'Sorry, I'm a bit dyslexic but I'll get there,' immediately changes the attitude of the person who's being impatient with you.

A lot depends on the way that you speak to the other person about your difficulties. If you seem confident and assertive, you're more likely to gain the respect and cooperation of that person than if you sound ashamed of your difficulties, or speak about them in an aggressive way.

I think it's true to say that the way you tell other people about your difficulties reflects the way you feel about them yourself. With luck, one result of an assessment will be to give you a good understanding of the situation. Then, when you discuss your difficulties with other people, you feel you are simply giving them useful factual information about yourself, and not revealing some 'guilty secret', or challenging them to a duel because they haven't been very helpful.

Spill the beans!
Do you feel embarrassed by your difficulties?
Do you feel people don't understand you?
Do people get impatient with you sometimes?
If so, it's time to tell them about your dyslexia!

COMMUNICATING EFFECTIVELY

What you need to do is speak to other people in an *assertive* way. Before giving some tips on this, we'll look at *unassertive* and *aggressive* ways of behaving so that you can compare these with the assertive way.

Unassertive body language
Lack of assertiveness can show in your body language. Try the following exercise to get a feel for unassertive body language.

Imagine a person is standing in front of you.

Stand up, then hunch your shoulders. Let your arms dangle awkwardly and shift your weight from one foot to the other. Bow your head and look downwards, occasionally darting an upward glance, but keep the head down. Look up for a moment and give a false, ingratiating smile, quickly followed by a frown. Cover your mouth with one hand for a moment, then let your hand fall again.

Notice how this body language makes you feel. Does it make you feel good about yourself?

Unassertive speech
You speak quietly and hesitantly with overlong pauses, or, by contrast, in a rushed and jerky way. You mumble and keep clearing your throat. You leave sentences unfinished and do a lot of 'umming' and 'erring'. You keep apologising and justifying yourself, and giving long, rambling explanations. You make self-critical statements, such as, 'I'm probably wrong, but . . .'; 'I'm sorry to take up your time, but . . .'; 'It's only my view . . .'

If your body language and style of speaking are unassertive, you are sending out strong messages of uncertainty and low confidence. You won't win respect or cooperation from other people, and you may well feel bad about yourself too.

Aggressive body language
Forcefulness, when taken too far, can be hostile and offensive, so avoid falling into this trap. Try the following exercise.

Imagine a person is standing in front of you.

Stand up with hands on hips and glare or stare fixedly in front of you. Jut out your chin and scowl. Lean forward, clench one fist and make jabbing movements with the fingers of the other hand. Pace angrily about the room.

Notice how this body language makes you feel. Do you feel this is a good way to communicate with other people and get their understanding?

Aggressive speech
You speak very loudly and emphatically. You use fast, clipped phrases with no pauses. While speaking, you make sharp hand gestures, such as thumping on the table. You stand very close to the person you are speaking to and lean towards them. You use provocative phrases, such as, 'That's stupid'; 'You're completely wrong'.

Having an angry rant might make you feel good temporarily, but, when you calm down, you'll probably find that this is all you have achieved. Again, you won't have won the respect and co-operation of the person you're talking to, and they may be even more unsympathetic to you in future. You'll be left feeling frustrated, and perhaps guilty, about your angry outburst.

So, when angry, punch a pillow in private and then consider how you might talk to people in an assertive, but not aggressive way.

Assertive body language
Try the following exercise.

Imagine someone is standing in front of you.

Stand up straight with your shoulders back, but not tight. Hold your head upright but not rigid. Look directly ahead without staring or glaring. Relax the facial muscles. Maintain regular but not constant eye contact with the other person. Move your hands and arms in an easy, relaxed way, suiting your gestures to the words you're using. Smile easily now and again. Have a good chuckle about something.

Notice how this body language makes you feel. Do you think it would make it easy for another person to interact with you and pay proper attention to what you say?

Assertive speech
You speak in a moderate tone, neither too loud nor too soft. You keep a steady, even pace, fluent, without hesitations. Your tone of voice

matches the content of your speech. You make short pauses between sentences, but not overlong pauses. You make assertive statements, such as 'My view is . . .'; 'I believe . . .'; 'In my opinion . . .'

If you cultivate assertive behaviour, you are much more likely to win respect and cooperation from others. And it will also help you to feel confident, competent and in control.

At this point you might think, it's all very well to say be assertive, but what if I don't *feel* assertive. What if I don't feel 'confident, competent and in control'?

Of course you can't suddenly switch from being unassertive or aggressive to being assertive and confident. But once you have gained an understanding of your difficulties, there can be a gradual change. And you can do some exercises to build up your confidence (see Chapter 12).

HOW PEOPLE REACT

The first effect of telling people you are dyslexic is usually that they start to show you a lot more sympathy and understanding. Often they feel quite relieved that they can now understand your difficulties and find ways to help you.

You may also find that telling other people about your difficulties in a calm and clear way has a very unexpected effect: you might help them to understand that *they* have similar difficulties. Dyslexia and dyspraxia do tend to run in families. It's not unusual, when a young person gets assessed, for one or other of their parents to read through the assessment report and have an 'aha' experience. That is, they suddenly say to themselves: 'But I've always had these same difficulties – I never realised you could do something about it.'

This is what happened in Paul's case. When his father read Paul's assessment report, he realised that he, too, had always experienced dyspraxic difficulties. So he went and had an assessment himself, and, as a result, got some help for his own problems. (One is never too old to have an assessment and get help – even grandparents do it.)

> An estimated 15 per cent of the population
> have some degree of dyslexia or dyspraxia.
> Not all of them know it.

In this book we are concentrating on ways in which you can help yourself, and you'll find plenty of suggestions about this in the next section.

CHAPTER 4 SUMMARY

In this chapter you learnt:
- ✓ How to explain your difficulties to other people
- ✓ How to speak assertively
- ✓ How to avoid speaking aggressively or defensively
- ✓ How telling other people about your dyslexia can help them as well as you

SECTION B

IMPROVING SKILLS

In this section of the book you will find suggestions and tips for improving your performance in all the areas that cause difficulty to dyslexic people. (As before, the information applies equally to those who are dyspraxic.)

In general you will need to:

1. Learn good strategies to help with underlying organisational, memory and perceptual problems.
2. Catch up on the basics of reading, spelling and writing.
3. Overcome mental barriers to progress.

There is a lot of information in this section, and it might seem difficult to take it all in, so I suggest you have a quick skim through the chapters first to get a general idea of their contents.

Then, over a period of weeks, concentrate on one chapter at a time, thinking about the advice given, deciding if it might be helpful to you and, if so, putting it into practice.

You don't need to work through the chapters in the order they appear in the book. Do them in the order you feel will be useful to you. However, *I do recommend that you start with Chapter 5*, on general organisational skills, as this will give you a good basis on which to work on all the other topics.

The sort of strategies you find helpful will depend to a large degree on the sort of learning style that suits you – that is, the way you find it easiest to learn things.

Some people have a verbal style, which means they learn best from written or spoken explanations, and from writing summaries or discussing their subjects with other people.

Others have a visual style: they use mind maps, diagrams, pictures, flow-charts, colours, imaginative layouts; or they visualise in their mind what they are trying to learn.

Many people have a mixed learning style, and make use of both verbal and visual strategies.

The important thing is not to classify yourself too rigidly as a verbal or a visual person, but to experiment freely and see what type of strategies help you with particular tasks.

As you start on the process of improving your skills, always remember that dyslexic difficulties do not detract in any way from your underlying intelligence, innate talents or actual achievements. Don't make the mistake of thinking that they do, and don't let other people make that mistake either.

CHAPTER 5

Organising Study

In this chapter we're going to look at a very basic and vital skill: being organised. Whatever you are doing, whether it's writing an essay, doing homework, planning a project, or simply getting yourself through the school day, you need to be well organised. I'm going to begin this chapter with some simple rules of good organisation, and then go on to look in more detail at particular ways of being efficient.

Four Golden Rules of Organisation
Plan and prepare.
Work in stages.
Take things slowly and steadily.
Take breaks.

---

1. PLAN AND PREPARE
This means:
- Knowing what you want to do
- Knowing when it has to be done
- Thinking in advance about how and when you're going to do it

Never skimp on planning. Even if you feel under pressure, and planning seems like one chore too many, you'll find that in the end you'll do things more quickly and more efficiently – and with less stress – if you plan them properly.

2. WORK IN STAGES
Take things one at a time.

Sometimes a task may seem daunting. For example, perhaps you have an essay to write. If you think about this whole task at once, it might feel overwhelming. You might find it difficult to get started, then if you manage to start, you might get disheartened and find your attention wandering to other things.

However, if you have planned the various stages of the work involved, you can calmly concentrate on one stage at a time – first the reading, then the planning, etc. This will make the whole thing more manageable and, again, less stressful.

It will also mean you work in an efficient way because you will be progressing through the tasks in a logical order, not darting from one activity to another.

3. TAKE THINGS SLOWLY AND STEADILY
Again, however pressed you are to finish some work, try not to tackle it in a rushed and nervous way. Be the tortoise, not the hare. If you rush, you will make mistakes, and it will all take longer in the end.

4. TAKE BREAKS
If you're rushing to get some work finished by a deadline, you might feel you haven't time to take rest breaks. But ponder this: research has shown that people who take short breaks usually

finish work more quickly, and get better results, than people who go grinding on, however tired they are. Tiredness, and the stress that comes with it, reduces your capacity to think, so in the long run it can take you longer to do things if you don't take rest breaks.

In setting out the Four Golden Rules, I used the example of essay writing. As Chapter 10 is wholly devoted to this important topic, the rest of this chapter looks at some general ways of organising your time and study schedule – always keeping the Four Golden Rules in mind.

ORGANISING YOURSELF

> Desk in a mess?
> Files lost?
> Lessons missed?
> It's time to get organised!

If you find yourself constantly in a muddle about *what* you should be doing *when*, if you keep missing deadlines and can never find the papers you need, it's time you got properly organised.

I'm going to suggest some basic items of equipment you should buy in order to get yourself organised. Then I'll explain how you can use each of these items effectively.

THINGS TO BUY
- Packets of large coloured labels – as many colours as possible
- A4 ring binders with dividers for each of your subjects
- Wallet to carry USB device or CDs
- Four A4 plastic trays in different colours
- Wall calendar to mark deadlines/appointments
- Notebook (small ring binder, preferably with loose-leaf sheets of different colours)

THINGS TO DO

This section tells you how to use the items of equipment you have bought. You might find it a bit confusing to read through this information before you have bought the equipment, so just skim through it for now to get the general idea. When you have bought the equipment, go through the section carefully stage by stage and follow the instructions.

Coloured labels

These will be used at various points in the organising process, so keep them to hand.

A4 ring binders

These are essentially your filing system, in which you will keep your notes and information sheets on all your different subjects.

Allocate one A4 ring binder to each of your subjects, e.g. French, history, physics. If possible, have a different coloured binder *for each subject*.

Label the binders, using your coloured labels (any colour), on the front, back and spine. Then, whatever messy heap your binders are in, you can easily see what you want.

Within each subject you'll have notes on particular topics. In history, for example, you might have Industrial Revolution, World War II, etc. Separate these in the binders with dividers. Label each divider with the name of the topic.

Combining paper and computer files

You may have subject notes both on paper and on the computer. You need to be able to 'marry' the two together efficiently, so you need to label computer folders and files to match the labels on your ring binders and dividers.

On the computer files you should do two things to help you identify things quickly. First, add a footer with an abbreviated form of the label at the bottom left of the page, e.g. HIST wor war 2. Second, insert page numbers at bottom right.

Then, if you do a print out a file, you can see at a glance what it is. And if you drop all your papers in a confused heap, or the wind blows them around the room, you can easily get them back in order again and file them in the correct section of the correct binder.

Wallet for USB device or CDs
Get into the habit of always carrying a wallet with your USB device or CDs so that wherever you are working on a computer – in the library, at a friend's house – you can transfer or back up any work you do.

If you have your own computer at home, make sure that *each evening* you transfer the information on the USB device/CDs to the correct files on your own computer. If, for example, you have copied some information on World War II from a friend's computer, this needs to be pasted into your file **HIST wor war 2**, not just left hanging around on the desktop.

A4 plastic trays
These are your action trays, each one with a different degree of urgency.
- Use four trays in different colours
- Make four labels (paper or cardboard) and stick or glue these on to the front of each tray
- Mark one label NOW
- Mark one label THIS WEEK
- Mark one label THIS MONTH
- Mark one label THIS TERM

When you come home from school and empty your bag:
- Put that evening's homework in the NOW tray
- Put anything you need to do during the rest of the week in the THIS WEEK tray
- Put anything that needs to be done during the month in the THIS MONTH tray
- Put anything that needs to be done before the end of term in the THIS TERM tray

NOW tray – Get into the habit of looking through the NOW tray – in a calm and collected way – both at the beginning and the end of the day.

In this way you can be sure you know what you are supposed to be doing that day, and at the end of the day you will check to see if you have actually done it.

You can make your end-of-the-day check simply by looking at the tray. If it is not empty, then something has been forgotten and needs to be done straight away, or given priority the following day.

THIS WEEK tray – At the end of the day, after checking your NOW tray, check your THIS WEEK tray. Is there something in it you want to tackle the next day? If so, put it in the NOW tray before you go to bed so that it will be given priority the following day.

THIS MONTH and THIS TERM trays – At the end of every week check your THIS MONTH and THIS TERM trays to see if there are things that need moving up the priority list. Something that has been THIS MONTH for a couple of weeks might now need to become THIS WEEK, and so on.

Wall calendar

Choose one that shows three months at a time so that you can see a term's commitments at a glance. Mark on the calendar all deadlines for essays, etc., and any appointments you make – meeting a friend, going to the dentist, and so on.

Meeting deadlines

It's important to schedule work carefully so that you meet any deadlines you have been set. Your wall calendar will help you with this. For example, once you've noticed you have a deadline for, say, an essay, you need to plan out how and when you are going to do the various stages of work needed to complete the project.

Keep the Four Golden Rules of Organisation (see page 43) in mind to help you with this. But now you need to think more precisely about just when you are going to put aside time to tackle the work. Here are the stages you will need to go through:

- Read the notes you already have on the essay topic
- Plan the structure of your essay
- Research further material, if necessary
- Write the essay
- Check your work to see if it reads logically
- Proofread your work for spelling and punctuation errors

How long do you estimate it will take you to do each stage? Let's say you estimate as follows:

Reading	5 hours
Planning	1 hour
Research	5 hours
Writing	3 hours
Checking/proofreading	1 hour

Altogether that adds up to 15 hours' work.

If your essay has to be finished in a month's time, you might want to find five hours of time in each of the three coming weeks to do the necessary work. That still leaves you a week at the end to give it a final polish.

Mark clearly on your wall calendar just when you are going to schedule the work. You could put aside one hour on each weekday, or do several hours at the weekend. Remember, though, that you may need to allocate some work to a time when the library is open.

Notebook

Use a small ring binder or personal organiser, preferably with loose-leaf sheets of different colours.

Keep this notebook with you at all times. It is your back-up memory. You will use it to jot down everything you need to remember – something a teacher or a friend has asked you to do, a useful thought that has occurred to you, a note of a book that sounds interesting, some instructions about homework – or anything else you want to remember.

Make the first section your ACTION LIST, and have further sections on IMPORTANT THOUGHTS, BOOK LISTS, HOME-WORK INSTRUCTIONS. The different sections can be in different colours.

The ACTION LIST is a vital section of your notebook. Throughout the day note down in it anything that needs doing. It might be something that someone has told you to do, or something you've suddenly thought of yourself. Put a large star against things you have to do that same day.

So your list might say:

Return books to library *

Get book on Macbeth for English essay

Mark essay deadline on calendar *

Phone John about cinema *

Buy more ring binders

Get into the habit of glancing through your ACTION LIST regularly. Once you have done a task on the list, cross it off clearly.

Let's say that by the time you get home in the evening, you've returned your books and phoned John. Your list would now read:

Get book on Macbeth for English essay

Mark essay deadline on calendar *

Buy more ring binders

Straight away you can mark up the essay deadline on the wall calendar and cross that item off your ACTION LIST. So you are left with two non-urgent things on the list:

Get book on Macbeth for English essay

Buy more ring binders

Try to do these as soon as you have a spare moment.

ORGANISING YOUR BAG

One last thing to organise: your school bag.

At the end of the day, think through the following day to see what things you should have with you when you leave for school. Any sports equipment? Particular textbooks? Work to hand in? Put everything you need ready in your school bag so that you don't even have to think about it the following morning.

Throughout this chapter, you have been given various times to check different things. Here they are, all together in a chart.

Check	First thing in the morning	Mid-morning	Lunchtime	Mid-afternoon	At home after school	End of the day	End of the week
NOW tray	✓				✓	✓ • The tray should be empty.	
ACTION LIST in notebook	✓	✓	✓	✓	✓ • Transfer that evening's homework to NOW tray. • Put other work/notes in appropriate trays. • Transfer any new computer disks/CDs (correctly labelled) to the correct files on your computer.	✓ • Should anything be starred for tomorrow?	
Calendar	✓				✓ • Any deadlines/appointments to add from ACTION LIST?	✓ • Anything scheduled for tomorrow?	

(Chart continued overleaf.)

Check	First thing in the morning	Mid-morning	Lunchtime	Mid-afternoon	At home after school	End of the day	End of the week
THIS WEEK tray						✓ • Does it contain anything that needs to be done next day? If so, transfer it to the NOW tray for action tomorrow.	
THIS MONTH tray							✓ • Does anything need to move to another tray?
THIS TERM tray							✓ • Does anything need to move to another tray?
School bag						✓ • Is it ready for tomorrow?	

PUTTING ORGANISATION INTO PRACTICE

Don't worry if you can't absorb all the information in this chapter at once. Just follow the Four Golden Rules (see page 43), working through things slowly and methodically at your own pace.

First, buy the equipment you need. Then read through the chapter again slowly, taking one section at a time.

Put aside a couple of afternoons to organise your materials. Do things one at a time:

- Decide where to keep your trays
- Get all your papers together and put everything in the proper ring binder or A4 tray
- Write out the binder and tray labels neatly
- Label your computer files to match your paper files
- Decide where to hang your wall calendar, and mark deadlines and appointments on it
- If you feel you're getting tired, take a break, then return to your task
- Work slowly and methodically until everything is done

Once you have everything organised, you simply have to follow your filing and checking routines from then onwards. Now you can feel sure that you will keep control of your workload: you will know exactly what you have to do, and when and how you are going to do it.

Finally, it can't be stressed too much how important it is to do this basic organisation work. Time spent on this now will save you hours and days of grief later. Try to get it sorted before term begins.

GETTING DOWN TO WORK

Some people find that, however well organised they become, they still have difficulty in actually getting down to work. They know what they should be doing, they have the correct books on their desk, but they keep putting off getting started.

If you find it hard to sit down and actually start studying, if you find a million things you *must* do before you start your homework, if you somehow manage to spend the whole evening on the telephone chatting to a friend, then you need to work out a little routine that will help you start work.

Set yourself a time at which you mean to start studying, say 6pm. Set a kitchen timer for that time.

When the timer goes off, leave or quickly finish off anything you are doing (and that includes phone calls). Go to your desk and set out the books and materials you need. Sharpen pencils. Line up coloured pens. Organise the lighting. Decide if you want music in the background. Put a DO NOT DISTURB sign on the door. Sit comfortably and give your hands and arms a bit of a shake to loosen them up. Decide how long you want to work for before you take a break: 30 minutes? 45 minutes? Set the timer accordingly. Take a deep breath and get started.

If your attention wanders while you are working, don't be anxious about it. Sit quietly for a minute or two just letting your mind rest, then resume work.

When the timer rings to signal the end of your work session, decide how much of a break you need. Take at least 10 minutes, but don't make your break too long or you might lose the thread of what you are doing. Set the timer for the time you want to restart work.

Always obey the timer. Start and stop work when it tells you to do so.

Another way to get things done without too much stress is to use 'odd moments'. Paul, for example, had a 20-minute bus journey to school. He used the time for reading his set books (he wore ear defenders so that he could concentrate). That meant he read for 40 minutes a day, which is over three hours a week, almost without noticing it.

CHAPTER 5 SUMMARY

In this chapter you've learnt how to:
✓ Label files
✓ Match paper files with computer files
✓ Keep back-ups of your work
✓ Keep track of what's urgent
✓ Meet deadlines
✓ Plan study schedules
✓ Keep a personal notebook
✓ Check what you need for school each day

For information on IT and technological aids to getting yourself organised see page 151.

CHAPTER 6

Memory

Memory is important in almost every aspect of our lives, so poor memory causes a host of problems.

You may recall from Chapter 2 that we have both a short-term memory and a long-term memory. In dyslexia it is short-term memory that usually causes a problem. In this chapter we'll look at strategies for giving your short-term memory a helping hand.

REMEMBERING IDEAS AND INFORMATION

If your short-term memory is poor, you may find that you can't quite remember what somebody has just said to you, or that you've completely forgotten a brilliant idea you had a moment ago.

This means you need memory 'back-up'. And the good news is that you already have this back-up in the form of your personal notebook with its separate sections (see page 49). So during the day, note down absolutely everything, important or trivial, that you will need to remember.

Taking the trouble to jot things down as they occur will leave you more clear-minded because it will take a workload off your memory. It will also relieve you from the stress of knowing there was something you had to remember, but not remembering what it was.

Do you forget . . .
what someone just said to you?
why you went into a room?
what you've read?
Then your memory needs help.

TAKING IN VERBAL INSTRUCTIONS

A particular situation in which your memory might let you down is when someone is giving you verbal instructions. For example:

'Please can you take these letters to the staffroom and ask one of the teachers to put them in the mail boxes. But this one to Mr Jones needs to be given to the secretary to post on to him. And on the way would you pop into the shop and get me six red folders and three blue ones. Oh – and a couple of pencils, the sort with erasers on the end. Oh yes, and can you tell the secretary to email Mr Jones about the theatre outing. Okay?'

Well, no . . . probably not okay.

To deal with a situation like this, you might need to show the sort of assertiveness we talked about in Chapter 4. You might need to ask the person giving you instructions to repeat them more slowly so that you can jot down the main points in your notebook:

letters ➜ staffroom mail boxes

tell sec: post let to Mr J and email him re outing

buy: 6 red 3 blue folders + 2 pencils with eras

If the other person seems impatient about all this, just point out or remind them that you are dyslexic and you need to take extra care with instructions. You will probably win their respect for making sure you get things right.

For longer sets of instructions, you could request having these given to you in written form, or you could record the instructions on a voice recorder or in an electronic diary.

If you do record things, note down straight away in your personal notebook what you have recorded so that you don't waste time later playing the recording backwards and forwards and trying to remember what's on it.

Numbers in a twist?
Names muddled up?
Notes full of holes?
Get some memory tips here.

REMEMBERING NUMBERS

You might have difficulty remembering numbers – telephone numbers, for example, or even short numbers, such as room numbers.

To remember a long number it's often useful to break it into sets of two or three digits. For example, look at the following number:

16032594

You break the number into twos:

16 03 25 94

Or you can use little tricks, such as noting if any of the combinations make up a date. In this case, you could take the first four numbers and say them as a date: 1603, and then just break the remaining numbers in twos:

1603 25 94

Or look for easy to remember chunks within the number and break the number around these:

    6812394 = 68 / <u>123</u> / 94
    33495707 = <u>33</u> / 495 / <u>707</u>
    29450006 = 294 / <u>500</u> / 06

To remember room numbers or street numbers, try using a visualisation technique. For example, if your teacher says your chemistry lesson is in room 17 today, think of that teacher with the number 17 flashing in bright lights on her head. Or imagine her at the age of 17 . . . A strong and incongruous image of something often fixes it in your mind.

REMEMBERING SEQUENCES

If you have difficulty remembering the alphabet, you could make an alphabet grid and keep it handy in your personal notebook. Use a different colour for each line of the grid:

A	B	C	D	E	F	G
H	I	J	K	L	M	N
O	P	Q	R	S	T	U
V	W	X	Y	Z		

You can do similar grids for the months of the year, or any other sequences you need to remember.

REMEMBERING LISTS

One way of remembering lists of things is to create associations for the items on the list, perhaps by putting them in a story.

For example, suppose you are trying to remember the names of the six wives of Henry VIII in the proper order. This is the actual order:

Catherine of Aragon
Anne Boleyn
Jane Seymour
Anne of Cleves
Catherine Howard
Catherine Parr

To remember the order, create a silly story about them with words that cue the queens' last names:

Henry VIII divorced his first wife, Catherine, because she was **arrogant**. He fell madly in love with Anne and rampaged about like a **bull in** a china shop until she agreed to marry him. But then he decided he must **see more** of Jane, until she too proved a disappointment. He then married his second Anne but soon decided to **leave** her. Next came the second Catherine, but she couldn't please Henry no matter **how 'ard** she tried. Out she went and in came the third Catherine. Henry was very happy with her and they had a **parr**fect marriage.

To remember the queens' first names in order, use the first letter of their names in a phrase, e.g:

Come **A**nd **J**oin **A** **C**onsort **C**lub

A 'consort', in case you didn't know, means a wife.

To remember what happened to the six wives this phrase might help:
- Divorced, beheaded, died
- Divorced, beheaded, survived

REMEMBERING TIMES TABLES

Keep a multiplication grid handy in your personal notebook. Colour different sections in different colours.

	1	2	3	4	5	6	7	8	9	10
1	1	2	3	4	5	6	7	8	9	10
2	2	4	6	8	10	12	14	16	18	20
3	3	6	9	12	15	18	21	24	27	30
4	4	8	12	16	20	24	28	32	36	40
5	5	10	15	20	25	30	35	40	45	50
6	6	12	18	24	30	36	42	48	54	60
7	7	14	21	28	35	42	49	56	63	70
8	8	16	24	32	40	48	56	64	72	80
9	9	18	27	36	45	54	63	72	81	90
10	10	20	30	40	50	60	70	80	90	100

To use the grid you need two rulers or two sheets of paper with straight edges.

Suppose you want to find the answer to 8 x 7.

Go down the left-hand side of the grid to the row that begins with 8 and place the ruler along the bottom of that row.

Then look along the top of the grid for the number 7, and place your second ruler to the right of that column.

Where the two rulers meet you'll find the answer to your sum: **56**.

RECALLING WHAT YOU HAVE READ

Short-term memory is very important in understanding and recalling what you read, especially if you are reading difficult textbooks. Strategies on remembering what you've read are discussed in detail in Chapter 8.

TAKING NOTES

Note-taking in lessons or lectures is a classic 'multi-task' activity. In simple terms, this means that, when taking notes, you have to keep several things in mind at once. You have to:
- Listen to the teacher
- Identify key points in what he/she is saying
- Write down the key points
- Be able to write down one point while listening to the teacher talking about the next point
- Recall what the teacher just said
- Keep your notes in a good structure
- Write legibly
- Maintain full concentration throughout

Teachers may provide printouts that show the structure of a lesson, or the content of any overheads they use. Always get one of these printouts before the lesson starts. Then you'll already have the structure and key points clear.

If the teacher doesn't provide a printout, you have a more daunting task ahead of you – a really big multi-task. Here's how you go about it.

You need to concentrate on two things:
- Following the basic structure of the lesson
- Noting down key words/ideas

Any well-prepared lesson will have a clear structure, and the teacher will probably give you signposts to the structure as he/she talks. Also, right at the beginning, he/she will often briefly summarise the content of the lesson.

Let's take an example from a history lesson.

The teacher comes in and announces that she is going to tell you about the causes of the English Civil War. At the top of the page where you will take notes, first write down your general label for the notes. In this case it could be:

HIST civ war

This is important because, as we saw in Chapter 5, you always need to have notes clearly and accurately labelled with overall subject and particular topic. Also, try to remember to number the pages as you write; or, even better, number and, if possible, label a few pages before the lesson starts.

Note that the teacher has said *causes* of the Civil War. This tells you that you will be listening out for a number of causes, which you will be able to number as you go along.

Now the teacher might start straight away by talking about causes. Or, more probably, she might begin with some general background about the period and the reigning monarch of the time, Charles I. In that case, begin by writing a heading BACKGROUND and then try to catch key points.

Listen out for when the teacher turns to the topic of causes. There will probably be a signpost. She might say something like: 'There were a number of reasons why Charles became unpopular. First of all, there was the question of taxes . . .'

So write on the left of the page:

C1 Taxes

C1 means cause 1. It's a good idea to use the letter C as well as the number 1 because there may be other sections of your notes where you have a list of numbers referring to something entirely different.

Try to get down the key points on taxes. But at the same time be alert for the teacher moving to another cause. She might say:

'Another area of difficulty for Charles was the religious question.'

So on the left you write:

C2 Religion

Again, try to note down the key points on religion while listening for further signposts.

Continue like this throughout the lesson. In this way, even if you don't take in all the detail, at least you've got the structure of the lesson and some basic information about the causes of the English Civil War.

You could also consider getting a voice recorder to record lessons so that you can listen to them through afterwards. (There's more information on this on page 152.) However, it is still *very important* to try to get the basic outline of the lesson and as much detail as you can during the lesson. Then you're not starting from scratch when you're listening to your recording. You will already know the main gist of the material that's coming up and you will be able to focus on the things you missed in the lesson.

Take notes faster
To speed up your note-taking, develop your own abbreviations for common words or particular subject words that you use frequently. For example:

rep	represent
repn	representation
conc	conclude
concn	conclusion
dif-c	difficult
dif-r	different
intro	introduction
argu	argument
purp	purpose
info	information
transn	transformation
ques	question
acc	according to

Start by building up a core group of 20 to 30 abbreviations for words you use very often. Read through the list regularly and try to use them a lot. When this group of abbreviations is firmly fixed in your long-term memory, gradually add to the list.

ELECTRONIC MEMORY AIDS

Various recording devices can be used to make notes and reminders for yourself. For information on electronic memory aids, see page 152.

CHAPTER 6 SUMMARY

This chapter gave you tips on remembering:
✓ Ideas and information
✓ Verbal instructions
✓ Numbers
✓ Sequences
✓ Lists
✓ Times tables
✓ What you have read
✓ What you hear (note-taking)

CHAPTER 7

Perception

If your perceptual skills are poor, you may find it difficult to analyse and understand complex visual material, such as maps, graphs, diagrams or tables of figures. You may have difficulty seeing letters in the right order and keeping your place when reading. You might have trouble presenting your work in a neat way.

Perceptual problems are often particularly marked in dyspraxia. In fact, some people define dyspraxia as 'perceptual and motor difficulties'.

The reason that many dyspraxic people have difficulties with maths is that it's a subject that requires good perceptual skills. It requires you, for example, to read equations accurately, deal with geometrical figures, analyse graphs and use a calculator.

Here are some tips on increasing your efficiency in perceptual tasks.

KEEPING YOUR PLACE WHEN READING

Some suggestions that might help you to keep your place are:

- Track down the pages with a pencil as you read
- Use a ruler to keep your line
- Cut out a 'reading window' in a piece of cardboard so that you can read one section of text at a time:

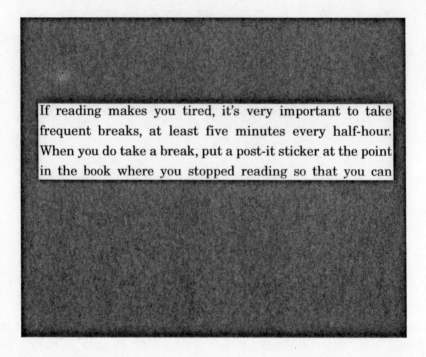

> If reading makes you tired, it's very important to take frequent breaks, at least five minutes every half-hour. When you do take a break, put a post-it sticker at the point in the book where you stopped reading so that you can

If reading makes you tired, it's very important to take frequent breaks, at least five minutes every half-hour. When you do take a break, put a post-it sticker at the point in the book where you stopped reading so that you can easily find it again when you resume.

DEALING WITH TABLES

Suppose you are shown the following table of figures in a textbook, and you are asked to copy it or to find a particular item in it.

Number of books sold by subject and by month											
	Jan	**Feb**	**Mar**	**Apr**	**May**	**Jun**	**Jul**	**Aug**	**Sept**	**Oct**	**Nov**	**Dec**
Fiction	340	298	361	403	561	648	732	754	613	439	480	675
Travel	128	187	295	390	561	548	649	671	549	457	428	547
Self-help	486	276	397	386	482	380	287	310	439	375	469	539
Science	207	430	384	297	205	307	387	370	301	298	387	398
Gardening	302	378	397	462	495	543	592	489	421	398	372	476
Music	391	403	497	375	429	348	401	328	364	402	456	502
Cooking	482	491	389	471	382	319	301	378	398	474	396	495
Arts	328	316	324	389	412	424	518	496	402	387	305	408
Media	343	296	301	359	372	334	405	368	324	397	288	362

It's easy to lose your place in a mass of figures like this, and to make mistakes. To avoid this, you need to put some structure on the table, to divide it up in some way, so that you know where you are in it.

Here are some ways of dividing up the table:

- Create columns. Rule vertical lines between each single column of numbers. Make every third line extra thick. Three-column chunks are easy to work with, as you always have a 'beginning, middle and end'. In this case, each three columns represents three months.
- Create sections. Rule horizontal lines under each row of figures. Under every third row, do an extra-thick horizontal line. Each three-row section represents three subjects.
- Colour each three-row subject section a different colour.
- Use two rulers, or two pieces of paper with straight edges, in combination to find a particular point in the table, such as the number of travel books sold in February (187) or the number of gardening books sold in July (592).

Number of books sold by subject and by month

	Jan	Feb	Mar	Apr	May	Jun	Jul	Aug	Sept	Oct	Nov	Dec
Fiction	340	298	361	403	561	648	732	754	613	439	480	675
Travel	128	187	295	390	561	548	649	671	549	457	428	547
Self-help	486	276	397	386	482	380	287	310	439	375	469	539
Science	207	430	384	297	205	307	387	370	301	298	387	398
Gardening	302	378	397	462	495	543	592	489	421	398	372	476
Music	391	403	497	375	429	348	401	328	364	402	456	502
Cooking	482	491	389	471	382	319	301	378	398	474	396	495
Arts	328	316	324	389	412	424	518	496	402	387	305	408
Media	343	296	301	359	372	334	405	368	324	397	288	362

If you are looking at a table on the computer, you can use the same sort of strategies. You can colour, embolden or italicise certain rows, or use different type sizes to create sections that are easy to distinguish.

If you are starting from scratch creating your own table, be imaginative in how you lay it out. For example, suppose you are listing kings of England up to Henry VIII with the dates of their reigns. How can you lay this out to help you consult it easily and remember it?

Here are the kings in question:

William I, William II, Henry I, Stephen, Henry II, Richard I, John, Henry III, Edward I, Edward II, Edward III, Richard II, Henry IV, Henry V, Henry VI, Edward IV, Edward V, Richard III, Henry VII, Henry VIII.

You could go dizzy just looking at that. Here's one suggestion for layout. Look up the date each king began his reign. Then divide the dates into groups according to which century each reign began. Then use a different colour for each century:

11th century	William I	1066
	William II	1087
12th century	Henry I	1100
	Stephen	1135
	Henry II	1154
	Richard I	1189
	John	1199
13th century	Henry III	1216
	Edward I	1272
14th century	Edward II	1307
	Edward III	1327
	Richard II	1377
	Henry IV	1399
15th century	Henry V	1413
	Henry VI	1422
	Edward IV	1461
	Edward V	1483 (three months)
	Richard III	1483
	Henry VII	1485
16th century	Henry VIII	1509

Also, if Roman numerals confuse you, you could write down the equivalent Arabic numeral next to the Roman one, e.g. Henry IV (4).

DEALING WITH MATHEMATICAL DATA

For ease of reference, the various types of data are dealt with under separate headings below.

READING NUMBERS ACCURATELY

You may find that you often reverse numbers, lose your place in long numbers or copy numbers incorrectly. Perhaps you always feel worried that you *might* have made a mistake with a number, so you spend a lot of time checking and rechecking.

In the last chapter, on memory, we looked at ways you could break up numbers to help you remember them (see page 57). You can use similar strategies for reading, checking or copying numbers accurately.

For example, you could adopt a policy of reading numbers in three-digit sequences, and checking each such sequence *once* before moving on to the next three digits. In this way

5968472059

becomes

596 847 205 9

Read the numbers out loud as you check them.

On the computer you can physically break the number up. In a textbook you own, you could mark off the three-digit sequences in pencil, or shade them in different colours. In a textbook you don't own, you could use a ruler or straight piece of paper to mark off three digits at a time.

ANALYSING COMPLEX VISUAL DISPLAYS

Complex visual displays could include diagrams, graphs, pie charts or bar charts. These types of data might include a lot of detail, and often the details are packed densely together in small print.

Here are some suggestions for dealing with this type of material:

1. Get an overview
Try to get an overview of the visual display before you by reading the main title, or the row and column headings and subheadings, or the titles of each axis on a graph, etc.

2. Make things easier to read
In general, follow the advice given earlier (see page 68) and use colours and lines to highlight and divide up the contents of a bar chart or graph. Look at the examples below:

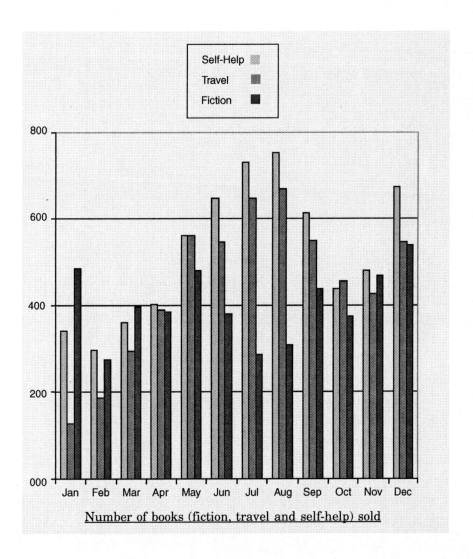

Number of books (fiction, travel and self-help) sold

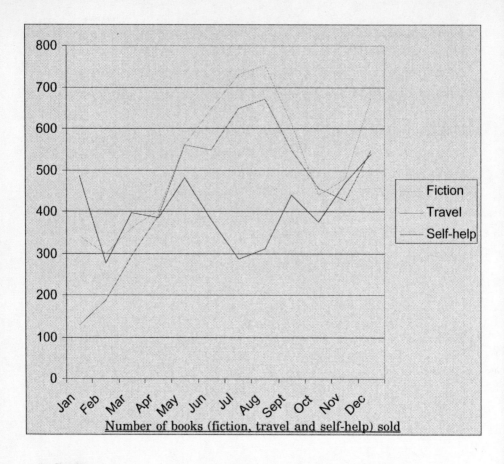

Number of books (fiction, travel and self-help) sold

3. Scan

For things such as tables of statistics, which do not present a clear visual overview or pattern, scan the diagram carefully and methodically from left to right and top to bottom (or along one column, row or section at a time).

Do not skip erratically from place to place all over the page, covering some sections more than once and others not at all.

Take in each piece of information separately.

4. Think about the data

It helps if you try to think about what is being presented: what it means, how each part of the display relates to other parts, etc. For example, in the graph above think about why sales might be low in certain months and high in others.

VISUAL STRESS

Some people suffer from a condition known as visual stress (sometimes also called Meares-Irlen Syndrome). They find that white paper seems to 'glare' at them, and that letters and numbers jump about on the page. They have difficulty looking at maps and at patterns that include a lot of straight lines. They see drawings or geometric figures as having fuzzy edges. Reading brings on headaches and eye strain.

Ways to deal with this are to cover the page with a coloured overlay or plastic file sleeve or to use a coloured reading ruler. This may reduce the glare and stabilise the image. If a major problem persists, however, an assessment should be arranged with an optometrist who specialises in colorimetry (see page 161).

ARE YOU SUFFERING FROM VISUAL STRESS?
If you place a tick against most of the questions below, you may be suffering from visual stress.

1. Does reading make you tired? ☐
2. Do you often lose your place when reading? ☐
3. Do you reread or skip lines when reading? ☐
4. Do you ever read words/numbers back to front? ☐
5. Do you miss out words when reading? ☐
6. Do you tend to mis-read words? ☐
7. Do you use a marker or your finger to keep your place on the page? ☐
8. Are you easily distracted when reading? ☐
9. Do you become restless or fidgety when reading? ☐
10. Do you get headaches when you read? ☐
11. Do your eyes become sore or water? ☐
12. Do you screw your eyes up when reading? ☐
13. Do you rub or close one eye when reading? ☐
14. Do you read close to the page? ☐
15. Do you push the page away? ☐
16. Do you prefer dim light to bright light for reading? ☐

17. Does white paper (or a white board) seem to glare?.... ☐
18. Does it all become harder the longer you read? .... ☐
19. Does print seem to jump about or blur?................... ☐

© Melanie Jameson

PARENT ALERT
If your child says . . .
print jumps about,
white paper glares and
lines float about on the page,
a colorimetry assessment may be useful.

Both Louisa and Paul were tested for visual stress. Louisa didn't have a problem, but Paul did, so he had an assessment with an optometrist, who prescribed glasses with tinted lenses.

Some people find these glasses very helpful, others don't. In Paul's case they were very helpful indeed. This is what he said about them:

'These glasses have made a huge difference to me. Now when I'm reading, the words stand out more clearly – before they used to sort of float about above the page. Also I'm less bothered by the bright white of the page.

'I've noticed the difference too at school with the lighting. It's a bit hard to describe, but I used to find the lighting in the classroom quite bright and upsetting. With the glasses it's much less glaring.

'I've also noticed I'm not so clumsy when I'm wearing the glasses. I can see the edges of things much more, so I don't bump into them. And when I'm drawing or painting I can see things much better.'

If you, too, have noticed the sort of problems that Paul talks about – print swimming around, white paper 'glaring' at you – there are a number of things you can try:

- Put a coloured file sleeve over a page of text and see if it makes any difference. Try lots of different colours to see which ones suit you.
- Experiment with background and text colour on the computer. You may find some colours much easier to look at than others.
- Photocopy textbooks or information sheets onto coloured paper.

In the last three chapters we've looked at general skills that dyslexic people need to work at: organising themselves, memory and perception. In the next three chapters we'll look at aspects of literacy skill: reading, spelling and writing.

CHAPTER 7 SUMMARY

This chapter has given you tips on:
✓ Keeping your place when reading
✓ Dealing with information presented in tables
✓ Reading numbers accurately
✓ Dealing with graphs or bar charts
✓ Dealing with visual stress

CHAPTER 8

Reading

Reading is a complex activity, but at its most basic it can be summed up as:
- Reading words accurately
- Reading text with comprehension and recall

In this chapter we'll begin by looking at ways of improving accuracy, and then continue with some advice on reading with good comprehension and recall.

READING ACCURACY

To read a word accurately, you have to:
- Recognise the letters
- Assign the correct sounds to the letter you've recognised
- See the letters in the correct sequence (visual tracking)
- Say the letters in the correct sequence (phonological sequencing)

This might sound simple, but in practice it often isn't. For example, take a long word such as:

incomprehensibility

There's many a person who starts off well with this word but grinds to a halt or descends into confusion in the middle of it. There are 19 letters to recognise, pronounce and sequence.

At this point you can call to your aid the organising skills that you learned in Chapter 5. You may recall the advice to break down tasks into stages. The same principle applies to reading long words. When closely analysed, long words are not just long strings of letters; they are built up of smaller units, called syllables. Each syllable is one or more letters that make a simple sound. An efficient way to read a word is to read it syllable by syllable.

See if you can find the syllables yourself in the word 'incomprehensibility' by singing it slowly to a well-known tune, 'Auld Lang Syne'. First, sing 'Auld Lang Syne' slowly with its real words. This will let you see that the longer words separate out into different notes. Each note is a syllable.

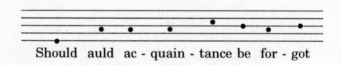
Should auld ac - quain - tance be for - got

You'll see that 'acquaintance' has three syllables and 'forgot' has two syllables.

Now try singing 'incomprehensibility' to the same tune.

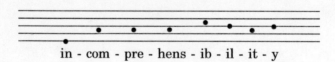
in - com - pre - hens - ib - il - it - y

As you'll see, it breaks down into eight syllables – an improvement on 19 letters.

One technical thing you might like to note about syllables: they always need to contain at least one vowel sound. Just to remind you, the five vowels are **a,e,i,o,u**. And note that the letter **y** can sometimes act as a vowel too.

If you look again at the syllables in *incomprehensibility*, you will see that each one of them contains either a vowel or the letter y.

Now practise singing some more long words to any tune you like. If you have access to a musical instrument, such as a piano or guitar, you could accompany yourself with it. Alternatively, simply drum out the rhythm of the word on a tabletop, count the syllables on your fingers or dance the word, doing one dance step for each syllable.

> If you recognise the parts, you'll understand the whole.

So try singing or dancing the following words to see how many syllables they have. (The answers are upside-down at the bottom of the page.)

complete
indefinite
reporting
incompatibility
extraterrestrial
unprepossessing
interdenominational

Once you get into the habit of splitting words up into their syllables, you will see that the same syllables occur again and again in many words.

Answers: 2 4 3 7 6 5 8

For example, take the first syllable of **in**comprehensibility. **In**numerable words begin with **in**.

Take the next syllable: **com**. This is a very **com**mon syllable.

Take the third syllable: **pre**. I **pre**sume you can find lots of words beginning with **pre**.

Finally, take the last three syllables together: **bility**. I'm sure you have the a**bility** to find this ending in many words.

These common syllables are called *prefixes* if they are fixed to the beginning of a word, *suffixes* if they are fixed to the end of it. Once you get familiar with these prefixes and suffixes (together called affixes), you will see that, when faced with a long word, you already know how to read most of its syllables. It's probably just the bit in the middle that won't be familiar to you, so you can concentrate on that. (We'll look more closely at affixes in the next chapter, which deals with spelling.)

So in order to read a text accurately, you really need to apply the Four Golden Rules of Organisation (see page 43), although on a much smaller scale:

- Prepare for reading long words by looking for familiar prefixes and suffixes.
- Read through the words one syllable at a time.
- Work through the words slowly and methodically; don't skip syllables.
- When reading a long text, take rest breaks.

What teenagers say
'It takes me hours to read things.'
'I never remember what I've read.'
'I never finish a book.'

READING WITH COMPREHENSION AND RECALL

Lots of people remark that their main difficulty is not with reading words, but with understanding and recalling what they have read. They spend long hours wearily reading things over and over again, desperately trying to understand and absorb the information given. The feeling that they're not taking anything in, despite all this effort, causes them stress and anxiety. The longer they read, the more tired and stressed they get, and the less they take in. It's a cycle of diminishing returns.

What's needed here is a more efficient reading *strategy*. Here are some suggestions:

1. Get an overview of the **structure** of the text before reading it in detail for content.

To do this:
- Note chapter headings, section headings and subheadings
- Make a summary of the overall structure

2. Now concentrate on the **content** of the text.

To do this:
- Go back and read the text in **detail**, taking one section at a time
- Keep your structure summary in front of you while you do this
- Highlight key words
- Then make notes on each section

3. Think actively about what you are reading.

4. Use **memory** strategies (association, visualisation, dramatisation).

5. Take regular **breaks.**

6. Review what has been read at regular intervals.

Now we'll look at these strategies in detail.

1. GET AN OVERVIEW OF THE STRUCTURE

Begin by skimming rapidly through the text to get an idea of its subject matter and direction.

If you are reading a whole book, start by reading the contents list, then look quickly at each individual chapter. Read the introductory paragraph to each chapter, which should give you an idea of its contents. Also read the concluding paragraph, which may give you a summary of the chapter.

If you are reading an individual chapter in a book, use a similar method. Note the name of the chapter to see what subject it deals with. Read the introductory paragraph and the concluding paragraph. Then skim through the whole chapter, noting any section headings or subheadings.

You can now make your own summary of the structure of the book or chapter. Please note: a summary of the **structure**, not the content. At this point you are not looking at the text in detail; you are simply noting the main headings or topics.

Let's take a chapter from this book as an example. Look back at Chapter 3, which deals with Assessment.

If you skim through this chapter in the way explained above, you can easily get an idea of its **structure** without knowing its content in detail.

Read the introductory paragraph. It introduces the main topic of the chapter: Assessment.

Look at the end of the chapter. The summary gives a rundown of the principal topics covered.

Go back and start skimming through the text. To get the overall structure, all you have to do is look at the section headings. When you find one, make a note of it on a separate sheet of paper. The first one you'll find in Chapter 3 is 'What's the purpose of assessment?'.

It might help if you label the headings with, say, a capital letter. So write down:

A. Purpose of assessment

The next is:

B. What happens in an assessment

But wait! Look at this section carefully. Within it you will see some subheadings in different weights or styles of type.

The first of these deals with the tasks mentioned at the beginning of section B, so let's indent it to show that it's a subdivision.

Assessment tasks

Now you come to several lighter headings, which relate to the bullet points on page 26 – a list of the tasks you do in an assessment.

So these are sub-headings in the Assessment Tasks section. To show this, write them indented slightly further and, if possible, in a different colour. And give them a letter. So now you have:

B. What happens in an assessment
Assessment tasks
- a. Reasoning
- b. Memory
- c. Perception
- d. Movement or motor skill
- e. Phonological skills
- f. Literacy skills

Next you will see text in a separate box about the emotions Louisa felt when she had an assessment. So, make this your next main point – don't indent it:

C. Emotional reactions (Louisa's account)

After this you will find one more main heading, which will be D in your list:

D. After the assessment

Now if you put all of the above together, you have a perfect outline of the chapter:

A. Purpose of assessment

B. What happens in an assessment
Assessment tasks
- a. Reasoning
- b. Memory
- c. Perception
- d. Movement or motor skill
- e. Phonological skills
- f. Literacy skills

C. Emotional reactions (Louisa's account)

D. After the assessment

Now that you have the structure clearly in view, you can move to concentrating on the content.

But before moving on to this, please note that there are many different ways of making notes on the structure of a text. Here we have simply presented the structure as a list. However, you could do it as a 'family tree' diagram or a spider map. (These methods are explained in detail in Chapter 10.)

2. CONCENTRATE ON THE CONTENT OF THE TEXT
As you begin to look at the text in detail, keep your plan of the structure in view. Then you'll always know whereabouts you are in the chapter, and how the part you are reading relates to what you have already read. Being clear about the structure of the chapter will free your mind to take in more of the meaning.

Let's take a subsection of Chapter 3 in more detail: section B.e. on phonological skills (see page 30).

While reading this subsection, concentrate fully on its topic – phonology – and don't let your mind dart about to other sections of the chapter. Also note how this particular subsection is structured.

You'll find two main types of information:

1. A reminder of what phonology is: recognising, pronouncing and sequencing sounds.
2. A description of relevant assessment tasks. Two types of task are described: reading nonsense words alone and in text, so you could label these 2a and 2b.

So your notes on this phonology subsection (using abbreviations) could be simply:

1. phon = recog, pron, seq sounds
2. tasks: read non words (a) alone (b) in text

The very act of making notes on the structure and content of the text will aid both your comprehension and recall of the material.

3. THINK ACTIVELY ABOUT WHAT YOU READ

It's important not just to let words wash over you when you're reading. If you do, you're unlikely to remember what they're telling you.

Consider carefully what you are reading, its meaning and purpose, how it links with other things, how it applies to the real world.

Question what you are reading, e.g. how useful it is, whether it makes sense.

Judge what you are reading, e.g. whether you agree with it, what its good and bad points are, what criticisms you might have of the ideas expressed, and whether you can think of better ideas.

Understand what you are reading. That is, don't lose the thread of the argument.

All this thinking forces you to make links between the text you are reading and other things you know. This enriches the memory trace of what you are reading, which is being put down in your brain, and makes it more likely that you will remember it later.

4. USE MEMORY STRATEGIES

To remember something, you need to make it vivid in your memory. You could do this through:

- Association
- Visualisation
- Dramatisation

Association

For an example of association, look back at the memory chapter (see page 59). Here you see how we aided recall of the sequence of Henry VIII's wives by linking their last names in a story, and by linking their initials in a phrase.

In the assessment chapter you could do something similar with the six topics in section B: **re**asoning, **me**mory, **per**ception, **mo**vement, **ph**onology, **li**teracy. Use the first letters in a phrase:

Really **me**morable **pe**ople **mo**ve **ph**enomenally **li**ghtly.

Visualisation

Imagine that you are going for an assessment. Look at the six types of task you will have to do and imagine yourself doing each of them. Which would be the hardest? Which the easiest?

Dramatisation

Even better, imagine you are the assessor. Visualise a rather nervous young person in front of you to whom you have to explain the six types of task. If possible, record yourself explaining the different tasks. Listen to your recording and think how you might have explained things better.

All the above techniques will help to put the content of the chapter in your long-term memory by making you go over the information several times and by giving you a vivid memory of it.

PARENT ALERT
Does your child hate reading?
Get audio books from the local library
or from postal libraries
(see page 159).

---

5. TAKE REGULAR BREAKS

On average the most efficient length of time for reading and remembering is between 30 minutes and an hour. The time will vary according to the ability of the reader, the difficulty of the text, the time of day, etc. It will be shorter than average for dyslexic people, who need to put more effort into reading.

When concentration does begin to flag, it's good to take a 10-minute break, or if this is not possible, to move on to a different, less arduous task for a while. You could get a kitchen timer and set the alarm to go off after 20 minutes, reminding you that you're getting towards the end of your efficient reading time.

6. REVIEW WHAT YOU HAVE READ AT REGULAR INTERVALS

It is good to review the notes on what you have read from time to time, as this will help lay down the information in your long-term memory. First, skim through the overview you wrote of the text structure. Then skim through any more detailed notes you took on the content of the text.

Other things that might help are reading a text aloud (though some people find this distracting), and finding an opportunity to discuss what you've been reading with fellow students. Again, the more you think about and discuss what you've read, the more likely it is to stay in your memory.

ELECTRONIC AIDS

You could invest in text-to-speech software, which scans in text and reads it to you. For language subjects you could buy tapes

of set books and listen to them when doing household chores –
yes, you *can* put romance and adventure into ironing!

For further information about software see pages 151–155.

CHAPTER 8 SUMMARY

This chapter gave you tips on how to:

Read accurately by:
- ✓ Breaking up words into syllables
- ✓ Recognising the beginnings of words (prefixes)
- ✓ Recognising the ends of words (suffixes)
- ✓ Recognising the middle of words (stems)
- ✓ Putting together the prefixes, stems and suffixes to read the whole word

Read with comprehension and recall by:
- ✓ Getting an overview of the structure of a text
- ✓ Getting an overview of the content of a text
- ✓ Looking at the text in detail
- ✓ Highlighting key words
- ✓ Making notes on the text

CHAPTER 9

Spelling

Perhaps, like many dyslexic people, you do not feel friendly towards the written word. Written words are things you can't spell. Things you can't read. Things you can't put together well in a sentence. Things that baffle you. Written words are the *enemy*, to be avoided if possible – to be wrestled with if they can't be avoided.

Do you remember Louisa, the dyslexic girl you read about in Chapter 1? Louisa used to say that when she looked at a long word in a book, it almost felt as if every letter in the word was a nasty gremlin, laughing and sneering at her and shrieking, 'Ha-ha-ha – you can't read me, you can't read me – you're stupid.'

But words don't have to be the enemy. If you got more familiar with them, more understanding of their habits, you might start to enjoy their company more.

To understand words better, you need to learn something about their structure. As we saw in the previous chapter on reading, words are not just random sets of letters thrown together in large quantities just to confuse you; they consist of recognisable building blocks.

In this chapter we are going to look more closely at the

structure of words in a way that will help both your spelling and your reading. You'll also be given a number of spelling tips. (It's beyond the scope of this book to offer you a complete spelling course, but if you take on board the advice given here, I think you'll feel more confident about spelling.)

SYLLABLES AND AFFIXES: A REMINDER

At this point, I would like you to leave this chapter for a moment and go back to the beginning of Chapter 8. There are two things there I would like you to look at again before continuing with this chapter.

1. SYLLABLES (SEE PAGES 78–80)
Here we saw how words are divided up into syllables. I asked you to try to sing or dance words in order to distinguish their syllables. Please practise this again now in the following way.

Pick up a book or a magazine that's lying around, highlight two or three sentences, then pick out the long words in these sentences. Sing, hum, drum on the table, or dance the words to separate out the syllables.

2. AFFIXES (SEE PAGE 80)
Refresh your memory about affixes. You need to be clear that there are two types: prefixes and suffixes. Prefixes go at the beginnings of words, e.g.

convertible

Suffixes go at the end of words, e.g.

convert**ible**

The bit of the word left in the middle is called the stem.

So here you have   prefix + stem + suffix

                           con   vert   **ible**

More about affixes

The first thing to note is that in the example above you have three 'building blocks', each of which can be used in many other words. Here are a few examples:

contain	in**vert**ed	poss**ible**
converse	di**vert**ing	terr**ible**
congregate	in**vert**ebrate	leg**ible**

The second thing to say is that there are many such prefixes and suffixes (and word stems) in the English language – many, but not an infinite number, so you can familiarise yourself with most of them. If you get so that you can quickly recognise them, you will be well on your way to reading and spelling long words accurately. Most long words are a collection of two or more affixes stuck onto a word stem.

A list of common affixes is given at the end of this chapter, along with an exercise to give you practice in recognising them.

A third point about affixes: they are not as meaningless as they might seem at first sight. Many of them have distinct meanings, and recognising these meanings will help you to recognise and spell the affixes – and hence words – properly.

Let's take two examples with prefixes. Look at the following words, which all begin with **re**:

re-enter	review
rewrite	return
repeat	restore

You can probably see that **re** in all these words indicates that something is done again. So you can say that **re** indicates *repetition*.

Here's another one, which you might need to think about a bit longer to see the meaning. Look at these words beginning with **con** or **com**:

conference   combine
congregate   compress
conversation   communicate

Perhaps you can work out that **con/com** have the sense of some-thing *going together with something else*. 'Conference' is where people talk *together*, 'congregate' is people coming *together*, 'combining' is putting things *together*.

Here are a few more prefixes with their meanings:

pre	in front of/before	preliminary, predate, prehistoric
un	not	unending, unlikely
extra	more than	extraordinary, extraterrestrial, extracurricular

See the affix list at the end of the chapter for more prefixes and their meanings.

Now let's have a look at some suffixes. These too have meanings. Can you see the meaning of **er** in these words?

painter
carpenter
writer

You probably deduced that **er** indicates a *person who does some-thing*, e.g. a painter paints.

Another common suffix, **ness**, appears in the following words:

happiness
wretchedness
restlessness

The meaning of **ness** here is something like *a state of*. So *happi-ness* means *a state of* being happy.

If you are very eagle-eyed, you might have noted that the word *restlessness* has actually got two suffixes. The stem of the word is *rest*. Then you add the suffix *less*, the meaning of which is obvious, to get the word *restless*, without rest. Then you add a second suffix, *ness*, to get *restlessness*, a state of being without rest.

So **restlessness** is best read *not* as 12 letters, but as three meaningful syllables.

rest-less-ness

More suffixes and their meanings appear in the affix list at the end of the chapter.

SPELLING NOTEBOOK

It's useful to keep your own notebook to note down spelling reminders, tips and rules. If possible, do this on the computer so that you can arrange entries alphabetically or in special groups. Print out the updated notebook regularly. Otherwise, use a small ring binder.

Here are some suggestions for the contents of your spelling notebook.

1. AFFIX LIST
A good start for the spelling notebook would be the list of affixes and their meanings given at the end of this chapter. *You don't need to put all of them into your notebook immediately* – that might seem overwhelming. Start with a dozen or so that you will be on the look-out for, and when you can reliably spot these, add a few more.

2. FREQUENTLY USED WORDS
There are probably certain words that you encounter again and again, but that you are never quite sure how to spell. They may be words that are generally very common, such as *friend* or *dependent*, or words that you use a lot in your particular subjects. In English, for instance, you might make mistakes in the names of authors, such as *Shakespeare* or *Dostoevsky*, while in maths you might have trouble with terms such as *rhombus, trapezoid* or *parallelogram*.

If you do notice the same words constantly giving you trouble, enter them in your spelling notebook. You could have separate sections for particular subject words, and then list other general words alphabetically.

3. WORDS WITH TWO POSSIBLE SPELLINGS

Some words have different spellings for different meanings. These words are called *homophones*. Keep a list of ones that continually trip you up. Use phrases or associations to help you remember which spelling goes with which meaning.

Here are two examples:

their – possessive, e.g. *their books*
there – place, e.g. *over there, not* here
they're – abbreviated form of *they are*

The sense of each becomes clear if you use them all in one sentence:

They're not there with their books.

stationary = at a standstill
stationery = used for writing letters (stationery has an **e** like 'email', also used for writing)

4. MEMORY JOGGERS

You can use little tricks to jog your memory about how some words are spelt. For example:

su**cc**e**ss**: A successful person has as much as possible of everything, so the word su**cc**e**ss** has as many **C**s and **S**s as possible

a**cc**o**mm**odate: Imagine you are trying to book accommodation at a hotel. You ask for two double rooms – that reminds you that you need a double **c** and a double **m**.

5. IRREGULAR WORDS

Irregular words are words you can't spell by the way they sound, e.g. tough, right.

You could collect groups of these:

tough	right	height
rough	might	weight
through	sight	freight
thorough	light	sleight

6. SUFFIXES WITH TWO POSSIBLE SPELLINGS

Some suffixes can be spelt two ways, and you can't tell from their pronunciation which way is right.

Here are some examples:

eat**able**	ed**ible**
writ**er**	auth**or**
depend**ent**	observ**ant**

There is no rule to tell you which is the correct spelling, so at the end of the day, you have to try to find a way to remember how these words *look*. That means really looking at them when you come across them.

There is something else you can do to help, though. With some of the pairs, one ending is much more common than the other. For example, **able** is more common than **ible**.

So you could have a section in your notebook where you write down the most common **ible** words. There won't be too many of them, so when you're not sure which ending is right for a word, you can quickly check through your **ible** list. If you don't find the word there, then the chances are that it ends in **able**.

Common words ending in -ible

edible	legible
incredible	divisible
possible	irresistible
feasible	horrible
terrible	audible

The same thing applies to the **er** and **or** suffixes. The **er** ending is more common, so you need to keep a list of common **or** words.

Common words ending in -or

author	tenor
actor	victor
professor	editor
conductor	tailor
director	sailor
impostor	inventor

---

7. LONG WORDS WITH SHORTER WORDS INSIDE THEM

Very often in long words there is a shorter word trying to get out. If you can spot the shorter word, you might find you know how to spell it, and it will then help you with the whole word.

For example:

irresistible

This is often spelt wrongly, e.g. irrisistable or irressistible or iresistable. But think for a moment: what does *irresistible* mean? It means something you can't *resist*. With luck you can spell *resist*, so that gives you the basis for spelling the whole word correctly. Add the prefix **ir**, then the suffix **ible**. You should get this right because *irresistible* is in your **ible** list above.

Can you find the short words hiding in these long words? The answers are upside-down at the bottom of the page.

sovereignty	disgraceful
courteous	discouragement
unprepossessing	disbeliever

Answers: reign, court, possess, grace, courage, believe

A USEFUL DOUBLING RULE

There are lots of spelling rules, and we can't go through all of them here. But I can give you one very useful rule that will help you to spell hundreds of words correctly. This is a doubling rule. It will help you to work out whether you need to double any letters when you add a suffix.

The doubling rule for word endings can be applied to:

- **Words** that end with a single consonant after a single vowel, e.g. beg*in,* cred*it*

Remember, the vowels are a, e, i, o, u.

- **Suffixes** that begin with a vowel,
  e.g. ing ed er or al ent ance

To understand how the doubling rule works, please go through the following steps one at a time. You'll need to use some of the things you learnt earlier in the chapter.

Step 1
Put the word and an appropriate suffix together and *say* the new word out loud. For example:

beginning   credited

Step 2
Listen to which syllable in the word is *stressed*, i.e. has more emphasis. Keep saying or singing the word till you can hear the stress. The stressed syllables in our examples are in italics below:

be *ginn* ing   *cred* it ed

If you have difficulty hearing the stress, try putting it on different parts of the word – the wrong stress will make the word sound silly, e.g. *be* ginn ing, cred it *ed*.

Step 3

If the syllable *before* the ending is stressed, double the letter before the ending.

be *ginn* ing

Otherwise, don't double:

cred it ed

Note: Words ending in a single l after a single vowel *always* double regardless of where the stress falls within them, e.g.

travel	expel
*tra*velling	ex*pell*ed

Here's some more to try for yourself. Cover the right-hand column while you do them.

prefer + ing	pre*ferr*ing
differ + ing	*di*ffering
remit + ance	remi*tt*ance
debit + ed	*de*bited
gossip + ing	*gos*siping
recur + ent	re*curr*ent
refer + ence	*re*ference
debug + ing	de*bugg*ing
rebut +al	re*butt*al
confer + ence	*con*ference

COMMON PREFIXES

Prefix	Meaning	Example
ad	to, towards	advance
con, com	together	companion
contra	against	contradict
de	down	descend
dis	not	disbelieve
ex	out	exterior
in, im	in, into	interior, implode
inter	among	international
mis	wrongly	mispronounce
mono	single	monopoly
per	through	pervade
poly	many	polysyllabic
post	after	post-war
pre	before	pre-war
re	again	review
sub	below	submarine
syn, sym	harmonious	synchronise, symphony
un	not	unhappy

COMMON SUFFIXES

Suffix	Meaning	Example
able, ible	capable of, fit for	eatable, edible
er, or	doer of an action	painter, director
ed	shows past time	called, shouted
ing	shows present time	I am reading
ess	shows feminine	lioness
ful	full of	fearful

ion, sion, tion	(1) state of	depress-ion, confusion, elation
	(2) event	explosion, election
ist	practitioner	chemist
ity	quality of	tranquillity
less	without	fearless
logy	study of	geology
ness	state of	happiness

PRACTICE IN SPOTTING AFFIXES

Take the affixes off the words below. Cover the right-hand column while you try this. As you do this exercise, think about the meaning of the affixes. The stems are shown in italics in the right-hand column.

distract	dis *tract*
intertwine	inter *twine*
monotone	mono *tone*
astrology	*astro* logy
calamity	*calam* ity
terrorist	*terror* ist
conversation	con *versa* tion
conversion	con *ver* sion
conservation	con *serva* tion
unbearable	un *bear* able
repression	re *press* ion
preparedness	pre *par* ed ness
submariner	sub *marin* er
persuadable	per *suad* able
discontented	dis con *tent* ed
reconvening	re con *ven* ing
statelessness	*state* less ness
interrelatedness	inter re *lat* ed ness
incompatible	in com *pat* ible

CHAPTER **9** SUMMARY

In this chapter you learnt spelling tips:
✓ A reminder about syllables, prefixes and suffixes
✓ The meaning of prefixes and suffixes
✓ Keeping a spelling notebook
✓ Dealing with words that have two possible spellings
✓ Memory joggers
✓ Irregular words
✓ Short words struggling to get out of long words
✓ A useful doubling rule

CHAPTER 10

Writing

You may find that you have plenty of thoughts and ideas, plenty to say to people, but when it comes to writing, you struggle to express yourself clearly and fluently.

Perhaps you experience a mental block when you sit down to write something – your mind 'freezes' and you just can't get started. Or perhaps the opposite happens: your mind fills with a jumble of ideas that you can't control or get into any order. If you do get started, perhaps you keep losing the thread of your argument and going off on tangents. And the more you keep rewriting your piece, the more muddled it gets, and the more tired you become . . .

Again, it's a cycle of diminishing returns.

Writing, however, doesn't have to be this painful. In this chapter we'll look at basic techniques you can use to plan, organise and structure written work in an efficient way. Then we'll look at ways of dealing with the mental block that can hinder you getting started with writing (see page 114).

Before we discuss planning, though, I need to remind you of the Four Golden Rules of organising any sort of work:

- Plan and prepare.
- Work in stages.
- Work slowly and methodically.
- Take rest breaks.

It's very important to observe these rules when doing any type of writing project: they will help you to keep a clear mind and avoid fatigue.

PLANNING WRITTEN WORK

When you are planning, say, an essay, you need to work through the following stages:

1. Focus on *exactly* what you are asked to write about.
2. Brainstorm for ideas.
3. Cluster and group your ideas.
4. Order and link your ideas.

When studying for your GCSEs or A levels, you may be asked to write essays in particular ways for different subjects. English, for example, needs a different approach from history. You can get detailed advice on this from GSCE study guides that you can find in any large bookshop. But don't forget: whatever type of essay you are writing, you need to think out its structure in advance, and to signpost your reader along the 'route' your essay takes.

1. FOCUS ON EXACTLY WHAT YOU ARE ASKED TO WRITE ABOUT
To illustrate this point, let's take a hypothetical essay with the following title:

Describe the range of difficulties denoted by the term 'dyslexia'.

Note that you have been asked to describe dyslexic difficulties in general.

You have *not* been asked to describe your own difficulties, or how you feel about the difficulties, or how annoyed you are that other people don't recognise the difficulties, or what help dyslexic people need.

You have just been asked to describe the difficulties.

2. BRAINSTORM

This is the creative stage – generating ideas for the essay. As ideas come to you, you need to jot them down quickly. But it's not helpful to jot them down any old how. You need to try and keep related ideas together.

There are various formats you can use to do this, including spider maps, 'family tree' diagrams and flowcharts.

For our essay on dyslexia, we'll use a spider map.

Take a blank A4 sheet and turn it widthways.

In the middle of the sheet draw a circle and inside it write the subject of the essay, i.e. dyslexic difficulties. You don't need to write this out in full; just put *Dys diffs*. (Remember to use abbreviations wherever possible.)

So you have:

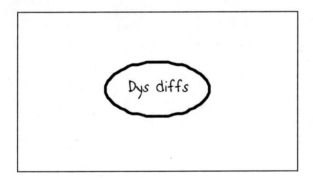

Now try to let ideas about this subject mill around in your mind. (If no thoughts come, look at pages 114–5, to see how you might encourage them.)

If you have an idea that seems relevant, quickly draw a line from your circle, draw a box at the end of it and write in a key word (or its abbreviation) for that thought.

For example, things that might occur to you – in no particular order – could be problems with: memory, reading, writing, organisation and spelling. So let's put these five things in boxes.

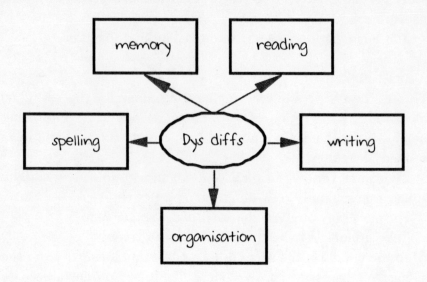

Perhaps you will have some ideas that you aren't sure are relevant. For example, is poor handwriting a dyslexic problem?

If you have an idea you're not sure about, don't just forget it. Do a separate box somewhere at the edge of the page and put that idea in it with a question mark.

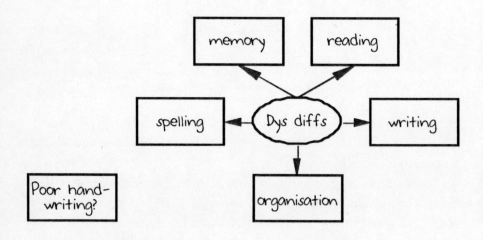

Leave that thought on one side for the moment.

Going back now to your main diagram. You have five boxes with different key words in them. Have a look at these again and think about them. Are they all definitely relevant to your subject? The answer, I would say, is yes.

Does anything else relevant come to mind? Perhaps it would be useful to subdivide some of these five topics.

Take the reading box, for example. Perhaps you'd like to mention two common types of reading problem: reading aloud and reading for comprehension. So add a couple of boxes to the 'reading' box and in them write 'aloud' and 'comp'.

Similarly, with writing, this might be subdivided into writing essays and taking notes. So add two boxes to the 'writing' box with the words 'essays' and 'notes'.

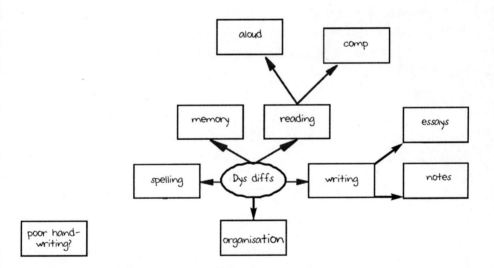

Now take a few more moments to look at the map and see if any more thoughts come to you. No? Then you have your essay content ready.

One last thing – you need to make a decision about the 'handwriting' box. Should you include handwriting in the essay? Is it perhaps more a dyspraxic problem than a dyslexic one? You could raise this point briefly at the end of your essay, as it would be relevant to mention that dyslexia and dyspraxia overlap. So leave that box where it is. If you find your essay is overlong, you could decide later to leave this point out.

3. CLUSTER AND GROUP YOUR IDEAS

So far you have thrown your ideas down on the page more or less just as they came to you. Now it's time to think about how you will arrange these ideas when you write the essay. Have a look at the five central boxes and see if any of them relates particularly closely to any of the others.

If I were writing this essay I might put reading, spelling and writing together, as these are all literacy skills. And I'd put memory and organisation together as non-literacy aspects of dyslexia.

To show this on the chart, colour-code the boxes accordingly. For example, use red for the reading, spelling and writing boxes, and green for the memory and organisation boxes.

Use red too to underline the sub-topics of reading and writing.

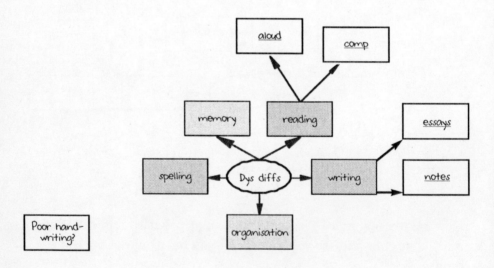

Now you can clearly see the main sections and sub-sections of your essay.

4. ORDERING AND LINKING YOUR IDEAS

Now you have grouped the various topics in a logical way, the next stage is to decide in which *order* you are going to write about them. In other words, make an essay plan. Look at all the topics you are going to deal with and think about a logical way to present them. Try out different plans until you feel satisfied.

Let's say you decide to start with the literacy skills and then move to the memory/organisation section. This would be quite a good order, as you're starting with the obvious dyslexic difficulties – reading, spelling and writing – and then moving on to the less well-recognised ones.

So your essay plan will be:

LITERACY:	reading:	1. aloud 2. comprehension
	spelling	
	writing:	1. essays 2. notes

MEMORY
ORGANISATION

WRITING THE ESSAY

If you have done your planning and preparation properly, you will be clear in your own mind about the structure and direction of your essay, but don't forget that your reader will be coming to it 'cold'. He/she will have no idea at all where you intend to go in your essay, so when you actually write the essay, it's important to give clear signposts to show both your main route (the boxes off the circle) and the side roads you are going to explore (boxes off the boxes). Otherwise you may lose your reader along the way.

INTRODUCTION

The first signpost you give your reader will be in the introductory paragraph to your essay. This will give a quick overview of the whole route you are taking (like a motorway sign saying simply THE NORTH).

In our essay on dyslexia, the introduction might be:

> In this essay I'm going to describe the main difficulties experienced by dyslexic people. I shall first talk about literacy difficulties, and then go on to discuss two other aspects of dyslexic difficulty: memory and organisational skills.

Note that you do not go into detail in the introduction. Usually a couple of sentences is enough.

MAIN PART OF ESSAY

Remember that every time you begin a new section or sub-section of your essay, you need to indicate this with a new paragraph.

So after your introductory paragraph, you will start another paragraph to begin the literacy part of the essay with something like:

> A dyslexic person experiences difficulty with all aspects of literacy skills, i.e., reading, spelling and writing.

Then signal each of these three topics in turn, as you deal with it, starting with reading:

> As far as reading is concerned . . .

A quick glance at your spider map will remind you that you are going to talk about two aspects of reading. You know that, but your reader doesn't, so let the reader know your intention right at the beginning by completing the sentence started above as follows:

> As far as reading is concerned, there are two aspects that often cause difficulty: reading aloud and reading with comprehension.

Then take the two aspects in turn, again signposting each one. Try to vary your signposts a bit – don't use the phrase 'as far as . . . is concerned' all the time, or your reader will fall asleep at the wheel. So, for example, you could begin the two sections with:

> Many dyslexic people will remember the horror of being asked to read aloud at school . . .

> Reading for comprehension is also an area of particular difficulty . . .

When you've finished saying what you want about reading, signpost your move to spelling.

> The second aspect of literacy I shall discuss is spelling . . .

And so on throughout the literacy part of the essay.

When you get to the memory and organisation part, you are making a major change of topic, so signpost the fact that you are leaving literacy and moving on to something different.

The literacy difficulties described above are perhaps the most obvious types of dyslexic difficulty. However, there are other aspects of dyslexia that, though less obvious, are equally troublesome, i.e. problems with memory and organisational skills.

Then signpost your way through these topics, just as you did with literacy.

Once you have gone through the sections of your essay, you will still have the handwriting box hanging about in a 'shall I/shan't I' sort of way. You could decide to refer to it in a couple of sentences, but because this topic is not in the mainstream of your essay, you need to make it clear why you are mentioning it.

So, *don't* just say:

Handwriting can also be a problem.

Relate it to the main topic:

Finally, it may be noted that dyslexia often overlaps with dyspraxia (difficulties with movement), so some dyslexic people also have dyspraxic problems, such as difficulties with handwriting.

Note that, as dyspraxia was a completely new topic in the essay, its meaning was explained in brackets.

When you reach the end of the main part of the essay, look back over what you've written to check that you have:

- Started each new point with a new paragraph
- Given enough signposts for readers to follow the direction of your thoughts easily

CONCLUSION

At the end of the essay you need to draw things together in a concluding paragraph. Whereas in the introduction you told the reader what you were *going to do*, in the conclusion you sum up what you *have done*. This means you might repeat the introduction to some extent, but it's good if you can also find some generalised 'rounding off' sort of remark right at the end.

So in our model essay, the conclusion could read something like:

In this essay, I've tried to show the full range of dyslexic difficulties and to demonstrate that these are not confined only to literacy skills, but also affect other areas of functioning, such as memory and organisational skills, the latter being important in all aspects of life.

ALTERNATIVE FORMATS FOR ESSAY PLANNING

In planning our dyslexia essay, we used a spider map with coloured boxes. However, not everyone finds this shape-and-colours approach helpful. They might prefer to jot down their ideas in a more linear form, that is to say, list the main points in a logical sequence.

If this would suit you better, you could list the ideas as we did in the note-taking section in Chapter 8.

Or you could use a 'family tree' diagram:

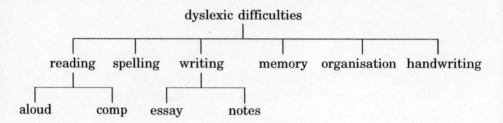

WRITING BLOCK

Writing is a task that dyslexic people find particularly stressful. However well you have planned and prepared an essay, you may still suffer from doubts and uncertainties when you sit down to write. You might feel sheer panic or revulsion at the thought of writing.

These negative feelings often show in your body language. Your muscles tense, your shoulders hunch up and you frown. With all this anxiety on top of the dyslexic difficulties, the flow of your writing can freeze up completely.

To lift the block, it's helpful to do a few minutes' relaxation before starting to write, or at any point where your writing 'freezes'. Just tense up your muscles for a moment, then let them relax. Repeat this 10 times.

Particular visualisations may also help.

Paul used to picture himself talking directly to the person who would read his essay. He imagined that person as nice and sympathetic. To reinforce this idea, he stuck up a large poster of a friendly-looking person on the wall in front of his desk at home, and imagined that he was speaking to that person whenever he had to write something.

Louisa used her imagination in another way. As she began to write, she imagined her mind as a huge dam, then visualised the flood-gates opening and the words pouring out.

Finally, if you find speaking easier than writing, you could try dictating to yourself. With your essay plan in front of you, speak your essay into a voice recorder. Don't worry if it's not perfect – just get the material out of your head and onto the recorder. Then play back your recording to yourself. Alternatively, you could use voice-activated software (see page 152).

HANDWRITING

It's not only structuring essays that can be a problem – actually writing them can be quite a labour too. Many dyslexic people, and particularly dyspraxic people, have poor handwriting and find it hard to write fast. As it is difficult to improve handwriting, it's best to type your work whenever possible.

One thing you could practise is writing numbers clearly so that you don't mix up, say, 1 and 7, or the number 5 with the letter S.

If your handwriting is very slow or difficult to read, you may be able to ask for the use of a computer in your exams.

ELECTRONIC AIDS

There is a wide and growing range of computer software and audio equipment that can help you with essay writing. This includes voice dictation systems and creative software. More details can be found on pages 151–155.

GENERAL WRITING TIPS

Keep the following tips in mind, and you will find essay-writing much easier.

STYLE
This applies to the words you use, the structure of your sentences and the layout of your work.

Keep it simple
Most subjects have some long technical words that you can't avoid using. But don't use long words if short ones will do.

Read the following sentence:

It is advisable when commencing upon the production of an essay to ensure that you have completed the necessary planning stage.

You could express this in three short words:

Plan your essay.

Always keep your reader in mind
Whom are you writing for (or to)? If you are writing an essay, then your 'reading public' will probably be teachers or examiners. You can write in a formal style, like the style of the essay we planned earlier.

But there may be other situations where you are writing for a very different audience. Suppose you are asked to contribute an article to the school magazine. You could write that quite informally:

'Hi - my name is Louisa and I'm writing to give you some tips on surviving school . . .'

You need to suit both your subject matter and style to your audience.

REVIEW YOUR WORK CRITICALLY
Have you included everything that is important? Have you started new topics with a new paragraph? Have you given enough signposts to the reader for him or her to follow the direction of your thought?

Signpost words
To indicate more on the same subject:
Secondly . . .
Finally . . .

In addition . . .
Also . . .
Furthermore . . .
Moreover . . .
Similarly . . .

To indicate contrast:
By contrast . . .
However . . .
Conversely . . .
On the other hand . . .
Nevertheless . . .

To indicate cause or effect:
Therefore . . .
Consequently . . .

To indicate time relationships:
Subsequently . . .
Previously . . .

PROOFREAD

When checking your work, keep the proofreading stage separate from the reviewing stage. In proofreading, you don't want to be distracted by the content of what you write. You need to concentrate on spelling, sentence structure and punctuation.

CHAPTER 10 SUMMARY

In this chapter you learnt how to go about writing essays, in particular:
- ✓ Focusing on exactly what you are asked to write about
- ✓ Brainstorming for ideas
- ✓ Clustering and grouping your ideas
- ✓ Ordering and linking your ideas
- ✓ Writing introductions and conclusions
- ✓ Dealing with writing block

You also learnt about:
- ✓ Different ways of planning your essays
- ✓ Writing styles
- ✓ Signposting your meaning to the reader

CHAPTER 11

Examinations

In this chapter we'll look at ways of scheduling your revision for examinations, preparing yourself mentally and practically for the exams, and actually taking the exams.

GETTING READY TO REVISE

If you have taken on board the advice about organisation given in Chapter 5, particularly the ideas for scheduling work to meet deadlines, you will be well prepared to organise your revision schedule.

STAGE 1: PREPARE YOUR MATERIALS

The first thing to do is to prepare what you need to work with. There are three principal things.

Your revision notes – again, if you followed the advice in Chapter 5, you will have all these clearly labelled and know where they are.

If you are missing some revision notes on certain topics and you need to borrow these from a friend or do some research in the library, write this on your ACTION LIST in your personal notebook.

Previous examination papers – your teacher will advise you where to get these from.

Revision schedule – put this on some A4 sheets that you can pin up on a corkboard or Blu-Tack to a door. This schedule will need to be visible at all times. (Stages 2 and 3 tell you how to prepare it.)

STAGE 2: DRAW UP A SYLLABUS LIST

Let's say you're taking six GCSEs and you want to start serious revision about five months before the examinations.

Go through your notes and previous examination papers and make a list of the main topics to be revised in each of your subjects. Under each topic, list sub-topics.

Let's take biology as an example. Your list might look as follows:

BIOLOGY

food

types	energy
nutrition	etc.

photosynthesis

overview	plant tissue
leaves	etc.
light	

If you divide your page into columns, you could get several subjects on one page so that you can see everything at a glance.

When you revise, take one sub-topic at a time. When you've dealt with that sub-topic, tick it off your list.

STAGE 3: DRAW UP A WORK SCHEDULE

Take an A4 sheet and mark it up as follows:

	Target Hours	Achieved
Monday		
Tuesday		
Wednesday		
Thursday		
Friday		
Saturday		
Sunday		

Photocopy or print out enough of these sheets to cover all the weeks in which you will be revising. Date each sheet accordingly.

At the beginning of each week, think through the week ahead to decide what is a realistic amount of time you can give to revision each day of that particular week. Don't make your targets too hard or too easy.

Use a pencil for marking up your schedule so that you can always change your mind as the week progresses.

If Monday is a busy day at school, maybe you can't fit in any revision. On Tuesday maybe you have a couple of free periods and could do about two hours. Write down your targets in the second column:

22 April–28 April

	Target Hours	Achieved
Monday	0	
Tuesday	2	
Wednesday	1½	
Thursday	1	
Friday	2	
Saturday	2	
Sunday	1	

At the end of each day mark in the 'Achieved' column the number of hours you have actually managed to revise. *It doesn't matter if you don't achieve your target every day*; the important thing is to aim for it. So don't think, 'Oh, I've failed.' Instead think, 'Well, I've got quite a bit done this week.'

STAGE 4: TALK THROUGH TOPICS WITH A FRIEND OR FAMILY MEMBER

A good way to make things stick in your memory is to discuss them with other people. So take some of your revision topics and talk them through with a schoolfriend, or give your family a mini lecture on the topics and invite them to ask questions.

PREPARING FOR THE EXAMINATION

In the run-up to the examination, practise answering some past exam papers. The exam will be much easier if you are already familiar with the style and format of the papers. In particular, be sure to practise answering multiple-choice questions so that you are in the habit of tackling these calmly and methodically.

Find out exactly where and when the exam takes place.

On the day before the exam, collect together everything you need to take to the exam:

- Pencil, preferably a soft one, for making notes on the question paper
- Eraser for rubbing out notes, if necessary
- Ruler to help you keep your place in a text or a grid

Make sure you have everything you are allowed, which might include a calculator, reference books, maths tables, etc.

Make a note of your candidate number and take it with you to the exam.

Give yourself plenty of time to get to the exam-room in time. Arriving in a panic-stricken rush will not help your performance.

Try to relax and feel positive before the exam. Take a few deep breaths before going in, and before starting to read your exam paper. Resolve to tackle things calmly, one step at a time. Imagine yourself keeping calm, remembering the facts and answering the questions well.

PARENT ALERT
Your child may qualify for
examination concessions, such as:
extra time
rest breaks
use of a reader
use of a scribe
transcription of papers
use of a computer

(Check with the special needs
coordinator at your child's school.)

TAKING THE EXAMINATION

Take things one at a time.

Be sure to enter your exam code, candidate number and any other information requested in the spaces provided on the exam paper.

Read the instructions on the exam paper *very carefully* before beginning to answer the questions so that you know:

- How many questions you have to do in total
- How many questions you have to do from each section
- How much time to allocate to each question

If you have a choice, choose the questions you think you can do best, and mark them on the exam paper with a tick so that you don't forget. Use a pencil for this. If you change your mind later about which questions to do, be sure to erase your original mark.

Then decide in what order you want to answer the questions (probably the easiest ones first). Then number the questions on the paper in pencil in the order you are going to tackle them. Try not to change your mind once you've chosen, but if you do change your mind, erase the original numbers.

Try to perform the above actions calmly and methodically. You need to have an overview of what you are going to do *before* you start writing.

If you 'blank out' or begin to panic during an exam . . .

- Stop writing for a few moments, and stop trying to force yourself to remember.
- Close your eyes and take several very deep breaths.
- Let your body relax, and allow your mind to feel clear and calm for a few moments.
- Briefly imagine yourself opening your eyes, remembering the facts, and feeling calm and controlled.
- Open your eyes and continue with the exam.

If you still can't remember the facts, go on to another question for the time being. Make a clear mark on your exam paper beside the incomplete question to remind yourself to come back to it later. The 'lost' information will probably come into your head a little later on. When it does, make a quick note of it to remind you when you come back later to complete the relevant question.

PARTICULAR TYPES OF QUESTION

Exam questions fall into approximately five different categories. We'll deal with each of these in turn.

ESSAY-TYPE QUESTIONS
Allocate a time for each question. Write down your time allocations on the exam paper.

Keep your eye on the clock so that you stick to the time allocations as closely as possible. If questions are of equal value, you might simply divide the total time by the number of questions. Or you might give more time to the more complicated questions, or to those you know most about.

Keep the exam paper (marked with your chosen questions,

the order in which you want to answer them and the time allocations) at the top of your desk where you can see it.

When answering the questions, work through them methodically – one question at a time, one stage at a time.

- Read each question very carefully before you answer it.
- Take note of the information that is requested. Highlight key words in the question to remind yourself what it asks.
- Keep the highlighted question in front of you as you plan and write your answer.
- Take note of what you are asked to do with the information (e.g. 'describe', 'discuss', 'explain', 'compare'). You will lose marks if you simply describe something that you were asked to 'explain'.

Don't assume that the examiners know anything. They are looking for what *you* know. Cover everything fully but do *not* write things that are not relevant to the question.

Where possible, and where relevant, try to show that you understand (as well as 'know') your subject. Show that you've thought about it.

Remember the clock. If time is running short, answer the questions you know well first, rather than spending time pondering over more difficult questions.

If you run short of time on the *last* question, jot down a rough plan, key words or brief notes. (It is possible to pass a question just on a good plan, but not for *all* the questions, of course.)

At the end, go back over your pages and check spelling and punctuation. Try to leave a little time for this.

STRUCTURED QUESTIONS
Look at the number of marks allocated to each question as you answer it (usually printed in brackets at the bottom right of each question).

If a question is worth two marks, only a few correct facts are required (though you may write a few more if you are not sure the points you've written are correct).

On the other hand, for a question worth 10 marks, a much longer answer is needed. Try to give at least 10 separate points, as elaborating on the same fact may not gain you extra marks.

QUESTIONS INCLUDING A PASSAGE OF TEXT

Allocate an amount of time to read the passage (e.g. five minutes in a 30-minute question).

Skim through the whole passage first to get the general meaning, and to notice the style and aim of the passage.

Go back and read the passage carefully. Think about each sentence as you read it; understand its content and purpose.

Visualise what you are reading about. This will bring it to life and help you to remember it.

MATHS QUESTIONS

Read the question carefully to see *exactly* what you are asked to do.

Show your workings as well as your answer, if required.

If the question contains a figure, chart or diagram, take the time to examine this in detail and think about it before answering the question (see Chapter 7).

MULTIPLE-CHOICE QUESTIONS

Read each question and possible answers *very carefully* before selecting the answer code.

If your answer options are in a grid, use a ruler to keep your place in the grid.

Initially, always use a pencil to mark the codes you select. This will allow you to rub out any codes you decide are wrong.

When you're sure about your answers, mark the correct ones in ink.

Be sure to mark your chosen code clearly and in exactly the right place so that there can be no doubt about which code you have marked.

The cardinal rule

Make sure you answer the question. When you're nervous it's very easy to misread things, such as Henry VIII instead of Henry VII.

Be sure you know what you are being asked to do. It helps if you know the precise meanings of the following words:

Analyse	Identify and explain the constituent parts of (i.e. break into bits, and explain the function/purpose of each).
Appraise	Judge the value/worth of.
Assess	*See appraise.*
Clarify	Explain more clearly.
Compare	Look for similarities *and* differences.
Criticise	Judge; present faults *and* good points.
Define	Set out the precise meaning.
Demonstrate	Show, by reasoning and examples, the truth of.
Describe	Give an account of.
Discuss	Talk about (i.e. explain, justify, analyse the arguments, evaluate).
Evaluate	*See appraise.*
Explain	Give reasons.
Illustrate	Use examples to explain/describe something.
Justify	Explain; give your own reasons for; support your view with evidence.
Outline	Describe, giving main features only.
State	Present in brief, clear form.
Summarise	State briefly the essential/main points.

EXAMINATION CONCESSIONS

If you have had an assessment that shows you to be dyslexic or dyspraxic, you could get concessions, such as extra time and rest breaks, in examinations.

In some cases you may also be allowed:
- A scribe (someone to whom you can dictate your answers)
- A reader
- Transcription of exam papers (if your writing is hard to read)
- Use of a computer

CHAPTER 11 SUMMARY

In this chapter you saw how to:

✓ Get ready to revise:
- prepare your materials
- draw up a syllabus list
- draw up a work schedule
- think through your revision topics

✓ Prepare for the examination:
- familiarise yourself with previous examination papers
- make sure you have the materials you need for the exam
- make sure you know the time and place of the exam
- do some relaxation exercises before the exam

✓ Take the examination:
- read the questions
- follow the instructions
- time yourself
- keep calm

✓ Answer particular types of exam question:
- essay questions
- structured questions
- questions including a passage of text
- maths questions
- multiple-choice questions

CHAPTER 12

Emotions

Dyslexia can be very upsetting. You may recall that Louisa and Paul, whom you met in Chapter 1, both said they felt despondent, frustrated and angry about their difficulties, especially when other people didn't seem to understand them.

What dyslexics say
'I feel intelligent and idiotic at the same time.'
'I get so embarrassed when I have to read aloud.'
'I'm always nervous I've made a mistake.'
'It's all so stressful and frustrating – I get so mad with myself.'

The negative emotions associated with dyslexia usually have the effect of making the dyslexic difficulties worse, and this sets up a vicious circle of inefficiency and anxiety. The good news is that if you learn better coping strategies for your difficulties, you will become more efficient, so any anxiety you feel will naturally decrease. You will also become more aware of your strong points, and hence more confident. However, it's important to have pro-active ways of managing the unpleasant emotions, and this is what we'll look at in this chapter.

First, let's take a close look at the emotions themselves.

CONFUSION

If you are dyslexic, you may feel confused about your true abili-ties. Louisa used to say that she felt intelligent and idiotic at the same time. When people told her things, she could catch on quite quickly, more quickly than other people. But in other ways she seemed slower than everyone else, and she made silly mistakes. So what were her abilities? She didn't understand herself, and no one else could understand her either.

EMBARRASSMENT

Life can be a constant embarrassment for a dyslexic person. You are asked to read aloud in class, and you make a complete mess of it. You fumble with your money in shops. You forget what you're saying to someone halfway through a sentence. You're given a form to fill in and can't make sense of it. The embarrassment makes the situation worse. Sometimes you might just walk away from a situation so as not to make a fool of yourself.

LACK OF CONFIDENCE

The feeling that you constantly experience difficulties with things that other people easily manage can deal a severe blow to your confidence and self-esteem. When you do a simple task, such as writing down a telephone number or writing a letter, you always have a nagging doubt: did I do that right? Over the years this constant self-doubt can colour the whole way you think about your-self. You come to feel that whatever you do won't be good enough. You ask yourself: among all these difficulties and inefficiencies, where is the person of worth? Is there a worthwhile me some-where?

FRUSTRATION AND ANGER

Dyslexic difficulties are very frustrating, and frustration can soon turn into anger. But it's not easy to know whom to be angry with. Your parents for not understanding the problem? Your teachers for not giving enough help? Your friends for telling you not to worry about it? But perhaps they all seem to be doing their best to support you, so in the end you might turn the anger on yourself.

STRESS AND ANXIETY

The confusion you feel about yourself, the worry about not doing things well, the embarrassment about making mistakes, the frustration about the situation – all these can leave you in a constant state of stress and anxiety. And then the anxiety about the difficulties becomes as much of a problem as the difficulties themselves. A vicious circle of anxiety and inefficiency is created, from which there seems no escape. Sometimes the anxiety intensifies into panic attacks that hit you in stressful situations, such as examinations. Or it may be expressed in physical symptoms, such as nausea, migraine and susceptibility to illness.

DEPRESSION

If you just go on and on in this whirlpool of emotion without getting any proper understanding and help, you could end up feeling seriously depressed. And this would be a perfectly natural reaction to a situation where you constantly seem to be struggling and striving without achieving the results you want.

RELIEF, DETERMINATION AND HOPE

So far this chapter seems to be full of doom and gloom. Yet all the emotions described above are commonly reported by dyslexic people, especially in cases where the difficulties have gone unrecognised for a long time.

However, once dyslexic difficulties have been recognised and strategies for dealing with them put in place, life can often take a turn for the better. All the energy that previously went into worrying about the problems and covering them up can now be channelled into developing effective ways of dealing with them, both practically and emotionally. In the rest of the chapter, we'll look at ways of doing just that.

Things *can* get better
You can . . .
improve your skills
build confidence
say goodbye to embarrassment
deal with stress and anxiety

STRESS REDUCTION

There are a number of techniques you can use to reduce stress and you may be surprised how effective they can be.

RELAXATION

In a particular stressful situation – take a few deep breaths, sit back and perhaps close your eyes. Take your mind away from the task or situation you are involved in. Continue to take slow, deep breaths in and out, focusing only on your breathing.

Imagine you're breathing in a stream of energy and clarity of mind. Feel the energy of the breath filling every part of your mind and body. Feel the out breaths as 'sighs of relief'. Imagine the anxiety as a grey mist, and breathe out a bit more of the mist with each breath, feeling the tension disappearing harmlessly into the air.

For long-term relief of stress – do regular daily relaxation or meditation exercises. There are many classes where you can learn and practise the basic techniques of relaxation and meditation. You can also buy one of the many audio tapes that give guided exercises. Usually the exercises combine bodily relaxation with techniques to relax the mind.

When you're stressed and overworked, it's easy to think you haven't got time to find 20 minutes for relaxation, but do find the time: it will make you more productive in the end.

A relaxation exercise is given at the end of this chapter.

VISUALISATION FOR RELAXATION

You can also reduce stress by using your imagination to visualise something peaceful and soothing. Imagine yourself sitting in a calm and tranquil setting, perhaps by a riverbank or on a secluded beach by the sea. As nagging thoughts come into your mind, just let the water carry them away.

Try to do this for 10 to 15 minutes each day. Always let yourself come out of the visualisation gradually: take a good 2 to 3 minutes to bring yourself back fully into your actual surroundings.

Again, you can buy audio tapes that will guide you through visualisations. You can also find a visualisation exercise for relaxation at the end of this chapter.

PHYSICAL EXERCISE

Taking physical exercise is a good way of giving the mind a break. Go for a jog, take the dog for a long walk, spend time in the gym or play a sport.

When working at the computer, it's particularly important to take a break for a couple of minutes every half-hour or so. Do some exercises that relax your neck, shoulder and arm muscles.

If you're sitting in a library and so can't move about, just tense up the muscles in your arms, hold them like this for five seconds, then let them relax. Do the same with your hand, neck, shoulder and facial muscles. Repeat this a few times. (Or you could retire to the loo for a quick work-out.)

PLAN AND PREPARE

Everyone, dyslexic or not, benefits by doing some advance preparation. (Remember Chapter 5?) So plan and prepare everything you do. Good planning puts you in control of the task you are doing, and this reduces stress and anxiety.

BUILDING CONFIDENCE

If you have had a dyslexia assessment, or if you have simply read through this book up to this point, you will be aware that you are much more than just the sum of your difficulties. You have all sorts of personal qualities and talents that need to be appreciated. So don't give yourself a hard time. Here are some things you could try in order to build up your confidence.

VISUALISATION FOR CONFIDENCE

Sit comfortably and begin to visualise an ideal image of yourself. Think of all the qualities you would like to possess – confidence, easy social manner, calmness, competence, clarity of mind. Imagine this 'ideal self' standing in front of you. Note his/her posture and facial expression: an upright, relaxed, confident stance, the eyes open and friendly, the gaze direct and confident.

Once the image of this ideal version of you has become reasonably clear, imagine yourself 'walking into the image' and becoming your ideal self. Begin to feel your own confidence and ability, your own clarity of mind, your own power and calm determination.

Next imagine yourself (in this ideal form) doing your school work or explaining something in class. Imagine yourself at some social occasion telling someone about your dyslexia in a calm and confident way.

Whenever you feel your self-confidence failing, bring to mind the image of your ideal self and *become* that person.

Of course, you can't suddenly become confident overnight, but there can be a gradual change.

TEST NEGATIVE THOUGHTS

If something has gone wrong, was it really all your fault? If you didn't understand an explanation, was it solely because of your dyslexic difficulties, or did the other person perhaps not explain things very well? Or did that person fail to take account of the fact that, being dyslexic, you might need to have something repeated?

If you are trying to explain something to somebody, and they seem to be impatient or miss the point of what you say, is that just because you haven't explained it well, or is it because they have something on *their* mind that has put them in a bad mood that day and made them feel distracted?

DON'T DWELL ON FAILURES
Brooding about failure consumes energy in useless worry and obstructs clear thought. So don't do it.

QUIETEN THE 'INNER CRITIC'
You may always feel that there is some critical part of yourself that seems to watch you and constantly put you down. Paul used to say he felt as if he had a little imp on his shoulder who was just waiting to laugh at him. Quieten this inner critic, in whatever form it appears, calmly but firmly. Don't be aggressive towards it because it is an unquiet part of yourself; just kindly but firmly tell it that it's going to have to revise its opinion.

ALLOW YOURSELF TO MAKE A MISTAKE
Everyone makes mistakes. Allow yourself a 'quota of mistakes', learn from them and move on to the next task without too much self-recrimination. In this way mistakes can be seen as 'teachers', rather than 'failures'.

POSITIVE AFFIRMATIONS
You may find that you often come up with negative remarks about yourself: 'I can't do that', 'I'll never get this essay done.' Such statements erode your confidence.

To balance them out, take time to think of some positive statements you could make about yourself. For example, you could say, 'I'm not stupid – I will be able to do this task if I use the right strategies,' or 'This might take me longer than most people, but I will get it done in my own time.'

COPING WITH ANGER AND FRUSTRATION

It's good to find ways of letting out anger and frustration occasionally, perhaps by punching a cushion. But please don't punch a person, as this will be counterproductive. Your angry feelings are justified, but you need to find ways to express them that don't do lasting damage to anyone, including yourself.

Two anger-busters from Paul
- 'Get a voice recorder and, when no one else is around, rant and scream your feelings into it. Listen to the recording and yell out agreement with everything you're screaming about.'
- 'Also get a small towel and give a door or solid piece of furniture a good slap around with it.'

If you do feel you are going to explode with anger in front of another person, try to pause for a moment and think how you can control the anger instead of letting it control you. Try to take the energy in the anger and divert it into a useful action.

For example, if you feel angry with someone because they do not understand or are not sympathetic to your difficulties, try not to lose your cool. Tell them in a calm but firm way that they are not taking account of the difficulties you are having to cope with. Point out that by being impatient with you they are making the difficulties worse. Offer to give them some information on dyslexic difficulties.

COPING WITH EMBARRASSMENT

There are bound to be times when you are embarrassed by your mistakes, or by other people's reactions to them. Louisa has some good advice about coping with this:

'I used to feel embarrassed in lots of situations – when I had to read aloud, when I didn't follow some instructions that a teacher gave me, when I got the letters in a word mixed up . . . the list was endless. But now I have a different attitude. I think to myself: why should I be embarrassed? I've got a few difficulties – well, people should give me a bit of sympathy and help. If they don't, *they* should be embarrassed, not me.

'With reading aloud, I just went to my teacher and asked her not to ask me to read aloud in class. I explained why – doing the whole calmly and firmly thing – and there was no trouble about it at all. In fact, she apologised for not having realised before that there was a problem.

'With instructions, again I just say to people very calmly, "Sorry, I'm a bit dyslexic. I need you to repeat that."

'The more I do this sort of thing, the more I enjoy it. I even look forward to situations where, instead of feeling embarrassed, I can give someone a bit of a lecture on dyslexia.'

COPING WITH DEPRESSION

If you feel despondent or seriously depressed about your difficulties, you'll know this is a very bad feeling. But don't feel bad about feeling bad. It's natural to be depressed in a depressing situation, and if you are depressed, it's hard to find the will and energy to lift yourself out of it.

Depression is usually connected with loss of hope. Perhaps you have come to feel that you have no hope of overcoming your difficulties, that they are a lifelong burden. *But this is not the case.* Most people manage very successfully to 'get round' their dyslexic difficulties, once they learn good strategies for dealing with them. It doesn't happen overnight, but it doesn't take years either. So begin, whenever and in whatever way you can, to work on strategies. If you simply feel too depressed to do anything at all, you should seek further help from your school counsellor or your GP.

EMOTIONS IN GENERAL

In this chapter we've looked specifically at emotions in relation to dyslexic difficulties. But, of course, distressing emotions can arise for any number of reasons. There may be factors in your life, apart from dyslexia, that make you feel angry, depressed or lacking in confidence.

In such a case, tackling the dyslexic difficulties will be a significant step forward because it will help you to understand and untangle at least part of your emotional problems. Then you will be able to see whatever is left more clearly, and concentrate on tackling those too.

Whatever difficulties you have, dyslexic or general emotional, try not to be on your own with them. If there is no one in your immediate circle you can confide in, look further afield. You could consult your school counsellor, your GP, or find help through a national counselling organisation for young people (see page 162).

To finish this chapter here are two relaxation exercises you can do. (You could record the instructions and listen to them as you do the exercises.)

Relaxation exercise

1. Pick a time when there will be no interruptions and switch on the telephone answering machine.
2. Sit comfortably.
3. Close your eyes and feel your body relaxing, sinking deeply into the chair like a rag doll thrown onto a cushion.
4. Tighten all the muscles in your legs and feet, then let them go suddenly and feel them relax. Feel all the muscles in the legs and feet becoming softer and softer, more and more relaxed, the legs feeling lighter and lighter, until they almost feel they are floating.
5. One by one, do the same with the muscles in the hands and arms, the stomach and the chest.
6. Tighten the neck and shoulder muscles. Release them and feel them going soft and loose.
7. Do the same with the jaw muscles. Feel the tongue resting gently in the mouth and all the face muscles soft and loose.
8. Feel the muscles around the eyes going soft and relaxed, the eyeballs resting gently in the sockets.
9. Feel your whole body, deeply relaxed, almost floating.
10. Gently turn your attention to your breathing. With each in-breath, feel peacefulness flow throughout every cell of your body. Feel a release of tension with each out-breath, like a 'sigh of relief'.
11. Just stay with the breathing for a little while, noticing its quality.
12. Thoughts will come to mind. Try not to engage them. Just let them fly by like a passing flock of birds. If you find yourself carried away in thoughts, don't get annoyed with yourself – just come calmly back to the breathing.
13. Gently bring the attention back to the body. Feel the chair beneath the body, and the firmness of the floor beneath the feet. Hear the surrounding sounds.

14. Gently stretch the arms, legs, shoulders and neck.
15. Slowly open the eyes and look around.
16. Take a minute or so to feel firmly back on the chair and in the room.
17. Always come out of the relaxation slowly and gently.

Ideally, this exercise should last between 10 and 20 minutes, and should be done twice a day, say, early morning and evening. It is best not to do it just before going to bed, as it tends to make the mind alert rather than sleepy.

Visualisation exercises for relaxation

You could include one or more of these exercises in the relaxation exercise above. If you do them separately, sit down, relax and close your eyes before beginning.

1. Imagine a stream of pure, sparkling, crystal-clear water flowing through the brain – in one side and out the other. Feel the purity and coolness of the water as it flows through the brain, cleansing it as it goes. Feel it washing away all the worries and fears and negative thoughts, leaving the mind fresh, clear and utterly relaxed. After a while, feel the flow of the water gradually slowing down until it forms a still, crystal-clear pool in the brain. Feel the surface of the pool becoming stiller and stiller, until its surface is like a perfect mirror.
2. Imagine the body as a factory closing down for the night. Feel all the workers leaving the factory – streaming out from the tips of your fingers and toes, and from the top of your head. Imagine the machinery shutting down, leaving the factory silent and empty. Feel a deep relaxation fill the mind and body as the factory falls silent.
3. Visualise a peaceful scene, such as a leafy forest with sunlight filtering through the trees, or a beach at night

with the moonlight reflecting on the waves, or a secluded garden on a warm summer's day. Use your imagination to see and hear and feel each detail of your chosen scene: the gentle breeze rustling the leaves and blowing softly against your skin; or the gentle breaking of the waves on the soft sand and the salty smell of the sea; or the scent and vivid colours of the flowers and the softness and smell of the grass. Be right there in the scene – feel yourself sink into the soft grass, or the sand, or a bed of leaves.

Remember, give yourself about 10 to 15 minutes to do the exercise, and 2 to 3 minutes to come out of it.

If you put into practice even some of the advice given in this chapter, I think you'll find that your dyslexic difficulties become more manageable. Although they won't go away altogether, they won't stop you doing what you want to do in life.

CHAPTER 12 SUMMARY

This chapter gave suggestions for coping with negative emotions:
✓ Confusion
✓ Embarrassment
✓ Lack of confidence
✓ Frustration and anger
✓ Stress and anxiety
✓ Depression

CHAPTER 13

Beyond School

When you leave school, you may go into further or higher education, or you may enter the workplace, or you may do both. Whatever you do, you will still need to manage your dyslexic difficulties because they don't just go away. And you will still need to make other people aware of your difficulties so that you can get proper help and support.

If you go on to college or university, you will probably find that there is plenty of understanding, sympathy and support for dyslexic students. In the workplace, however, awareness is much more patchy: many employers don't understand what dyslexia is or know how to deal with it. Below is some information that might be useful in these situations.

HELP IN FURTHER AND HIGHER EDUCATION

As soon as you know you have a definite place at a college or university, contact the disability officer or dyslexia support tutor at your college and ask what procedure you should follow to get help for your difficulties.

If you are at a college of further education, the college should have funds to give you tutorial support, and you should get extra time, and perhaps the use of a computer, in examinations.

If you are at a college of higher education, such as university, then you will get the help mentioned above, and you will also be able to apply for the Disabled Students Allowance (DSA). This provides funds for you to buy such things as computers, voice recorders, etc. You also get an annual general allowance for books and photocopying, and an annual 'non-medical helpers' allowance, which you can use to pay for things such as IT training, dyslexia tuition or a helper to type or proofread your work.

To get the DSA you should apply to the education department of your local authority. If you haven't already had a dyslexia assessment, you will need to get one now, either from a chartered psychologist or from a specialist dyslexia teacher who is accredited to do assessments. The disability/dyslexia officer at the college of your choice will be able to help you arrange this. (Some universities fund the assessment – always ask.)

Once the local authority has your assessment report, you will then go on to the next stage, which is called the Needs Assessment. This doesn't involve any tests; its purpose is to specify exactly what sort of help and equipment will be useful to you.

To learn where to find more information about dyslexia in further and higher education, see page 162.

HELP IN THE WORKPLACE

As a dyslexic person in the workplace, you have rights under the Disability Discrimination Act (DDA). An employer has a duty to make what are called 'reasonable adjustments' if a disabled (and that includes dyslexic) person is at a disadvantage compared to non-disabled employees.

Adjustments could include:
- Allowing you extra time to do things
- Giving you time off work for training
- Giving you a quiet workspace
- Providing relevant IT support

- Backing up oral instructions with written ones
- Helping you organise your work schedule

It's not just when you're in the job that an employer has to be sympathetic. The law also requires that adjustments are made when you're making your application for a job, or going for interviews.

For example, an employer needs to allow for the fact that your poor short-term memory might make it difficult for you to express yourself clearly in an interview, and that you might need a bit of extra time to think out what you want to say.

Also, if the application for a job includes some form of testing, particularly timed written tests, it's important to consider whether doing written work to a deadline will actually be part of the job. If not, it might be possible to waive the written tests in the application process. If you do have to do written tests, you could get extra time, or have someone to read the questions to you.

One thing that can be tricky when you apply for a job is that you need to decide whether or not you're going to tell the employer right from the beginning that you are dyslexic. Some people don't want to – either because they feel embarrassed about it, or because they think their difficulties won't be severe enough to impede them in their job.

However, it's important to note that if you don't tell potential employers from the beginning that you're dyslexic, they may not be legally obliged to make reasonable adjustments later on. In practice, however, most employers don't go by the book in making such decisions.

If you are applying for a job and are worried about your dyslexic difficulties, you could make an appointment to see the Disability Employment Adviser (DEA) at your local Job Centre Plus. The adviser will be able to explain your rights to you, give you advice on how to approach employers, and perhaps even arrange and fund an assessment. It may also be possible for the Job Centre to provide some funding for training through the Access to Work scheme, which is designed to help disabled people in employment.

To learn where to find more information about dyslexia in the workplace, see page 162.

CAREER CHOICE

People often ask what type of job or career is best for a dyslexic person. There is, however, no simple answer to this. A number of factors need to be taken into account:
- Your interests
- Your overall ability level
- Your pattern of strengths and weaknesses
- The severity of your difficulties
- How well you have compensated for your difficulties
- The amount and quality of help available to you
- Your determination to succeed in a particular sphere
- Your emotional state
- The demands of particular jobs or courses of study for professional qualifications

Some professions would be daunting – for example, if you have severe dyslexic difficulties you might find it hard to cope as a barrister, a job in which a large amount of reading often has to be done in a hurry. However, if your difficulties are mild and you have good compensatory strategies in place, you might cope.

It is sometimes assumed that all dyslexic people will have strengths in non-verbal fields, such as art or design, but this is a dangerous assumption. The fact is that everyone is different. You might be a gifted artist, but you might equally feel you have no particular gift at all. You'd just like to be doing better than you are at present.

In general, the best advice is to do what you're interested in and ensure that you have the best possible help and support.

CHAPTER 13 SUMMARY

This chapter gave information about:
✓ Dyslexia at college
✓ Dyslexia in employment
✓ Career choice

Endword

I hope you have found the information and advice given in this book helpful. I hope, too, that you remember the advice given right at the beginning, which was not to try and put all the recommended strategies into place at once, but gradually to build up a bank of them. Also, do try to get some help from a specialist dyslexia teacher if you can.

Finally, always remember that you are not defined by your dyslexic difficulties. You are your own person, with your own abilities, talents and personal qualities. The better you can manage your difficulties, the more you can realise your true potential.

You might like to know that both Louisa and Paul are well on the way to achieving their ambitions. Louisa has a place at drama school, and Paul is planning to train as a journalist – he is already doing some work experience on the local newspaper. Louisa and Paul both worked hard and were fortunate in getting some specialist dyslexia help. So in the end they got the better of their difficulties, rather then letting their difficulties get the better of them.

It remains only for me to wish *you* all the best for your future – at college, in work and in life generally.

Good luck!

SECTION C

FURTHER HELP AND ADVICE

In this last section of the book you will find advice on buying IT and other useful equipment, and details of organisations which give help and support to dyslexic and dyspraxic people. There are also suggestions for further reading.

Useful Equipment

In this section you will find general information on IT and technological support for people with dyslexic difficulties. The equipment discussed can help to improve your efficiency in various aspects of school work and in life generally, but there are certain things to bear in mind before making a purchase.

The first thing to note is that price is not always an indicator of usefulness: the most expensive items may not be the right ones for you.

It is very important that you seek up-to-date information and impartial advice on your particular requirements. Most of the general advice given on the Internet is useful, but you really need to consult personally with a specialist in the field (see page 161). Try to get a hands-on demonstration or a free trial of software before purchasing anything.

Please note that on certain items you might be able to apply for VAT relief. Consult the supplier.

ORGANISATION EQUIPMENT

Personal digital assistants (PDAs) are hand-sized organisers that work like mini-computers. They can store your diary, set alarmed reminders for appointments, create 'to-do' lists, store pictures, record notes and messages, and store documents for reading and editing wherever you are. You can synchronise your PDA with your PC to keep your diary and files up to date.

Caution: The battery life of some PDAs, particularly those with large, coloured screens, can be quite limited. If the battery is not kept charged, you could lose all the information you have stored.

If you don't have a PDA, there are some useful tools available within Microsoft Office, which is often pre-installed on your computer. Microsoft Outlook, for example, has a simple-to-use calendar/diary function with audible alarm.

SPEECH-RECOGNITION EQUIPMENT

There are software packages that allow you to dictate into your computer and have your words appear on the screen. The text can then be edited and printed, using, for example, Microsoft Word. The software also has the ability to transcribe voice recordings from digital recorders and PDAs.

Caution: Seek advice on which speech-recognition package is right for you. Some packages concentrate on each individual word as it is spoken, while others prefer continuous dictation. Your choice of package will depend on your dictating style.

TEXT-TO-SPEECH EQUIPMENT

These programs convert text to speech: they can read out loud practically any text that is on the screen. Hearing what you have written read back to you often helps with proofing your work. Web pages and other documents that you might be using for research are virtually transformed into 'talking books'.

SCANNING EQUIPMENT

Optical Character Recognition (OCR) software can scan printed documents and convert them into text documents on your PC. You can then read the document on your computer screen in the colour and format that suits you best: perhaps in larger print, with double spacing, or using different coloured backgrounds and print.

Use a scanner in conjunction with text-to-speech software to have the documents read aloud to you.

NOTE-TAKING EQUIPMENT

You can use a digital voice recorder to 'jot down' notes and reminders to yourself, which can then be 'transcribed' into a text document on your computer using speech-recognition software.

Caution: Make sure you choose a recorder that has a long recording time and can be connected to a PC.

You can also record instructions, conversations, discussions, lessons or tapes/CDs borrowed from the library, and then take notes at your leisure from *your* recording. Note that speech-recognition software is trained to understand your voice only, so it will only be able to transcribe notes you record yourself; it will *not* recognise the voices of other people speaking in lectures, classes, etc.

TYPING-TUTOR EQUIPMENT

Being able to type confidently, accurately and quickly will free your mind up to concentrate on the content of what you are typing. There are several computer-interactive typing tutors that will give you training in touch-typing.

SPELLING EQUIPMENT

Make sure you are making the best use of the spell-checkers that come as standard within, for example, Microsoft Word, Excel and Access. There are also sophisticated add-ons to word-processing packages that offer phonetic and homophone spell-checkers, and word prediction.

Hand-held spell-checkers are also available. These include a portable hand-held 'reading pen' that scans and displays printed words, reads and spells them out loud, and offers definitions from its in-built dictionary.

ESSAY-PREPARATION EQUIPMENT

You can plan and structure essays using computer-generated 'spider maps'. At the click of your mouse, these maps can be converted into text and exported to your preferred word-processing package. You can then edit the text using the keyboard or voice-recognition software, and finally proof it with the help of a screen reader.

COLOUR-SENSITIVITY EQUIPMENT

Microsoft Windows operating systems allow customisation of your computer with tools designed to help users with disabilities. For example, changing screen and font colours can reduce eye strain and prevent text from 'swimming' on the page. These functions are, however, limited and you might prefer to buy a specialised piece of software that can change all Windows colours, including the background colour, default text colour, menu background, text colour and toolbars.

When reading books or papers, you could use coloured overlays to stabilise the words. Professional overlays are available from Cerium Technologies (see page 161) and eye-level reading rulers from Crossbow Education (see page 161). To keep your place on the computer screen, use a screen reading ruler, e.g. from Textic (www.textic.com).

USE YOUR EQUIPMENT WELL

Choose a chair that supports your back. Don't slump on a sofa or work with a laptop on your knees.

Don't sit too close to the screen. If possible, have the screen at right angles to the light source.

If you find that working on a laptop causes strain or discomfort, consider buying an external full-sized keyboard and mouse that you can plug in. An ergonomic keyboard (designed for comfort and ease of use) is a wise investment as it encourages good posture.

GENERAL ADVICE ABOUT PURCHASING HARDWARE AND SOFTWARE

If you already own a computer, don't purchase any software until you've checked with the supplier that it's compatible with your equipment.

When purchasing a new computer, think carefully about the pros and cons of laptops and PCs. Laptops are easy to carry around, but they cost considerably more than a desktop PC, and are easily damaged or stolen. If you're keen to stay up-to-date, buy a desktop system because they are much easier to upgrade than laptops.

Most importantly, before buying anything, get up-to-date advice on all your hardware and software requirements. And be aware that much of the specialist software described in this section cannot be bought through high street stores.

For expert advice about dyslexia-friendly hardware and software see page 160.

IT TRAINING

To find local trainers, consult your nearest branch of the British Dyslexia Association (see page 157).

Try to arrange several short sessions of training rather than trying to master everything in a single intensive session.

Useful Addresses

All the following organisations offer general help and advice.

Bangor Dyslexia Unit
University of Wales, Gwynedd LL57 2DG
Tel: 01248 382 203
Email: dyslex-admin@bangor.ac.uk
Website: www.dyslexia.bangor.ac.uk
This branch covers the whole of Wales.

British Dyslexia Association (BDA)
98 London Road, Reading, Berks RG1 5AU
Tel: 01189 668 271
Email: helpline@bdadyslexia.org.uk
Website: www.bdadyslexia.org.uk
For list of all local associations, click on Information.

Dyslexia Association of Ireland
1 Suffolk Street, Dublin 2
Tel: 01 6790276
Email: info@dyslexia-ie
Website: www.dyslexia.ie

Dyslexia Association of London
Dyslexia Resource Centre, The Munro Centre, 66 Snowsfields,
London SE1 3SS
Tel: 020 7407 0900
Email: dal1449@btconnect.com
Website: www.dyslexiainlondon.ik.com

Dyslexia in Scotland
Stirling Business Centre, Wellgreen, Stirling FK8 2DZ
Tel: 01786 446650

Email: info@dyslexia-in-scotland.org
Website: www.dyslexia.scotland.dial.pipex.com

Dyslexia Parents Resource
Website: www.dyslexia-parent.com
Gives contact details for all BDA local associations.

European Dyslexia Association
Website: www.bedford.ac.uk/eda/members.htm

International Dyslexia Association
Website: www.interdys.org

DYSLEXIA ASSESSMENT AND TUITION

It is important that assessment and tuition are carried out by chartered psychologists or teachers who are dyslexia specialists and who have experience of working with the 13–20 age group. Consult your local branch of the British Dyslexia Association (see page 157) or the Dyslexia Institute (see below) for advice.

Dyslexia Action
Park House, Wick Road, Egham, Surrey TW20 0HH
Tel: 01784 222 300
Email: hqreception@dyslexiaaction.org.uk
Website: www.dyslexiaaction.org.uk

Dyslexia Teaching Centre
23 Kensington Square, London W8 5HN
Tel: 020 7361 4790
Email: dyslexiateacher@tiscali.co.uk
Website: www.dyslexia-teaching-centre.org.uk

Helen Arkell Dyslexia Centre
Frensham, Farnham, Surrey GU10 3BW
Tel: 01252 792 400
Email: enquiries@arkellcentre.org.uk
Website: www.arkellcentre.org.uk
Covers Surrey, Hampshire, Southwest London.

Independent Dyslexia Consultants
1–7 Woburn Walk, London WC1H 0JJ
Tel: 020 7383 3724
Email: info@dyslexia-idc.org
Website: www.dyslexia-idc.org

London Dyslexia Action
2 Grosvenor Gardens, London SW1W 0DH
Tel: 020 7730 8890
Email: london@dyslexiaaction.org.uk
Website: www.dyslexiaaction.org.uk

PATOSS (dyslexia tutors oganisation)
PO Box 10, Evesham, Worcestershire WR11 6ZW
Tel: 01386 712650
Email: patoss@evesham.ac.uk
Website: www.patoss-dyslexia.org

DYSLEXIA SUPPORT

Among the audio libraries that offer a mail-order service are:

Calibre
Website: www.calibre.org.uk

Listening Books
Website: www.listening-books.org.uk

To make friends and compare notes with other dyslexic people
you can log on to:
iamdyslexic.com
learningstyles@aol.com (penpals)

DYSPRAXIA SUPPORT

Developmental Adult Neuro-Diversity Association
46 Westbere Road, London NW2 3RU
Tel: 020 7435 7891
Email: mary@pmcolley.freeserve.co.uk
Website: www.danda.org.uk

Dyscovery Centre
4a Church Road, Whitchurch, Cardiff CF14 2DZ
Tel: 02920 628 222
Email: info@dyscovery.co.uk
Website: www.dyscovery.co.uk

Dyspraxia Association of Ireland
69a Main Street, Leixlip, Co Kildare
Tel: 01 295 7125
Email: info@dyspraxiaireland.com
Website: www.dyspraxiaireland.com

Dyspraxia Foundation, The
8 West Alley, Hitchin, Herts SG5 1EG
Tel: 01462 455016
Email: admin@dyspraxiafoundation.org.uk
Website: www.dyspraxiafoundation.org.uk

Teenagers Dyspraxia Connexion
21 Birchdale Avenue, Hucknell, Notts NG15 6DL
Tel: 0115 963 2220
Email: notts@dysf.fsnet.co.uk
Website: www.dysf.fsnet.co.uk

IT ADVICE AND TRAINING

AbilityNet
PO Box 94, Warwick CV34 5WS
Tel: 01926 312847 or 0800 269545 (helpline freephone)
Email: enquiries@abilitynet.org.uk
Website: www.abilitynet.org.uk

Dyslexia in the Workplace
Flat 2, Grafton Chambers, Churchway, London NW1 1LN
Tel: 020 7388 3807
Email: workplacedyslexia@btopenworld.com

Iansyst Training Project
Fen House, Fen Road, Cambridge CB4 1UN
Tel: 01223 420101
Email: reception@dyslexic.com
Website: www.dyslexic.com

To find a local consultant, check with your local branch of the British Dyslexia Association (see page 157).

VISUAL PROBLEMS – COLORIMETRY ASSESSMENT

Colorimetry assessments are not done in standard eye tests; contact the Dyslexia Research Trust (below) for a specialist in your area.

Barnard Associates
58 Clifton Gardens, London NW11 7EL
Tel: 020 8458 0599
Email: sb@eye-spy.co.uk

Cerium Visual Technologies
Tenterden, Kent TN30 7DE
Tel: 01580 765 211
Email: ceriumuk@ceriumvistech.co.uk
Website: www.ceriumvistech.co.uk
Manufactures tinted overlays and can provide a list of colorimetry specialists in your area.

Crossbow Education
Website: www.crossboweducation.com
Sells eye-level coloured reading rulers

Dyslexia Research Trust
University Laboratory of Physiology, Oxford OX1 3PT
Tel: 01865 272 116
Email: info@dyslexic.org.uk

Institute of Optometry
56–62 Newington Causeway, London SE1 6DS
Tel: 020 7234 9641
Email: admin@ioo.org.uk
Website: www.ioo.org.uk

GENERAL COUNSELLING

Childline
Tel: 0800 1111
Website: www.childline.org.uk

Connexionsdirect
Tel: 080 800 13219
Text: 07766 413219
Textphone: 08000 688 336
Website: www.connexions-direct.com (including webchat)

Young Minds
102–108 Clerkenwell Road, London EC1M 5SA
Tel: 020 7336 8445
Website: www.youngminds.org.uk

FURTHER AND HIGHER EDUCATION

Advice for students at: www.dyslexia-college.com
and www.skill.org.uk

WORKPLACE

Dyslexia Adults link
Website: www.dyslexia-adults.com

Working with Dyslexia
Website: www.workingwithdyslexia.com

Job Centre Plus
Website: www.jobcentre.plus.gov.uk/cms.asp
Offers advice on coping with disability in the workplace.

Further Reading

General Interest
The Adult Dyslexic: Interventions and Outcomes, David McLoughlin, Carol Leather, Patricia Stringer (Whurr Publishers, 2002)
Dyslexia and Stress, ed T. R. Miles (Whurr Publishers, 2004)
The Dyslexic Adult in a Non-dyslexic World, Ellen Morgan and Cynthia Klein (Whurr Publishers, 2000)

For Students
Dyslexia at College, T. R. Miles & D. E. Gilroy (Routledge, 1995)
Use Your Head, Tony Buzan (BBC Books, 2003)
Includes many techniques for improving the memory.

For Teachers
Dyslexia in Secondary School, Jenny Cogan and Mary Flecker (Whurr Publishers, 2004)
Dyslexia and the Curriculum.
A series of books covering individual GCSE subjects (British Dyslexia Association/ David Fulton, 2003, ongoing).

For People in Employment
'Briefing Paper 6 on Dyslexia in the Workplace', Employers Forum on Disability
Nutmeg House, 60 Gainsford Street, London SE1 2NY
Tel: 020 7403 3020
Website: www.employers-forum.co.uk
Dyslexia in the Workplace, Diana Bartlett & Sylvia Moody (Whurr Publishers, 2000)
Dyslexia: How to Survive and Succeed at Work, Sylvia Moody (Vermilion, 2006)

Dyspraxia
Living with Dyspraxia, ed Mary Colley (Jessica Kingsley, 2006)

Index